Pasta Salad Light

Pasta Salad Light

Nina Graybill and Maxine Rapoport

Farragut Publishing Company
Washington, D.C.

First printing 1995
PRINTED IN THE UNITED STATES OF AMERICA

Library of Congress Cataloging-in-Publication Data

Graybill, Nina.
Pasta salad light / Nina Graybill and Maxine Rapoport.
       p.   cm.
ISBN 0-918535-21-2
1. Cookery (Pasta) 2. Salads. 3. Low-fat diet—Recipes. 4. Low-calorie diet—Recipes.
I. Rapoport, Maxine. II. Title.
TX809.M17G6823   1995
641.8'22—dc20   95-11119
                                                                            CIP

Cover photogragh by Renee Comet

For Barry, yet again.
N.G.
For the Barczak brothers — thanks for always being there.
M.R.

Introduction

*I*n 1984 we published the very first book devoted solely to pasta salad, THE PASTA SALAD BOOK. It was the beginning of the great Pasta Renaissance when Americans discovered to their delight that pasta dishes didn't have to be weighty and fattening, like lasagne or macaroni and cheese. In place of rich, heavy sauces, pasta salad offered crunchy vegetables and fruit, tangy dressings, and interesting new ethnic flavors. With pasta salad one could eat well — and eat right, too.

The response to the book was enthusiastic, for all the reasons we expected. Pasta salads are remarkably versatile; they are usually easy and economical to prepare, and can be made in advance. They are sophisticated enough to serve to guests, yet so convenient and satisfying they can be brownbagged to the office. There are recipes refreshingly suitable for hot weather or warm and hearty for winter.

However, we were intrigued by the compliments THE PASTA SALAD BOOK received from the nutrition- and weight-conscious, from athletes, and many others who watch what they eat. They loved the taste and the good nutrition of pasta salad. But they wanted help in cutting still more fat and calories from the recipes.

We hadn't written THE PASTA SALAD BOOK as a diet book, and while some recipes were low in fat and calories, others definitely were not. Many studies in recent years have advocated more complex carbohydrates and fiber, and less fat (especially saturated fat), in the diet. Pasta salads certainly offer these benefits, but we saw many possibilities for improvement without jeopardizing the taste and character of the original recipes.

Hence this book. PASTA SALAD LIGHT contains many of the dishes you loved in THE PASTA SALAD BOOK. We've reduced the fat by substituting low-fat or no-fat products wherever possible. The amount of oil used in dressings has been reduced — after all, the difference between half a cup and a quarter cup of olive oil is 470 calories and 54 grams of fat. Dressings have also have been lightened with broth, fat-free yogurt, low-fat sour cream, and low-fat mayonnaise. In some cases we use less meat, and substitute low-fat cheese for regular cheese.

In some recipes we've not only changed the ingredients in a sauce, but reduced the amount as well. If this leaves the salad less moist than you like, add a little vegetable or de-fatted chicken broth just before serving to achieve the consistency you prefer for very little added fat or calories. Also, you will notice in many recipes we call for the use of olive oil or canola oil. Both are mono-unsaturates. Feel free to use all of one or the other in any recipe. While we like the taste of olive oil, canola may be your choice.

A wakeup call for every pasta enthusiast came in February 1995 as we worked on our manuscript. The headline in *The New York Times* read: "So It May Be True After All: Eating Pasta Makes You Fat" and went on to explain that in about one in five people, starches may cause the body to produce more glucose, and thus more insulin, which may then cause storage of more glucose as fat. Many authorities have since disagreed with the broad generalization drawn by this news report. Nevertheless, the story serves to remind all of us that what we eat with our pasta — and how much — has a lot to say about weight gain.

It is always important to keep in mind the difference between "low fat" and "low calorie." Pasta, which is virtually fat-free, has about 100 calories per dry ounce, or about 400 calories in an average serving. So if you are concerned about calories as well as fat, consider increasing the amount of vegetables called for in any recipe. The complex carbohydrates and fiber in the fruit and vegetables are filling, and, combined with pasta, will leave you feeling satisfied, not deprived.

We didn't try for sainthood with PASTA SALAD LIGHT. Many of our low-fat recipes have at least some fat for a more luxurious flavor. We also kept our sausage recipes, which may shock or surprise some of our readers. But we love it, and and wanted to continue to enjoy the marvelous flavor of pasta salad combinations with sausage. We have reduced the fat in these recipes by using less meat, using turkey or veal sausages which contain less fat, and substituting low-fat cheeses. Our fellow sausage enthusiasts can enjoy this occasional treat — but we do not pretend these dishes are fat-free.

The nutrition headlines vary from day to day. But the cumulative wisdom suggests it is hard to go wrong by increasing our intake of fruits and vegetables — complex carbohydrates and fiber — and reducing fat. The other fundamental lesson surely is that there is no magic solution to a good diet: not a vitamin pill, not a single food, nor, for most of us, a rigid adherence to a joyless, pallid regimen in which eating is a chore.

The keys, after all, are common sense, moderation — and enjoyment. All are present in abundance in PASTA SALAD LIGHT.

Pasta Salad Tips

As with any type of salad, quality and freshness count. Use pasta made from semolina or durum wheat flour — it holds its shape and texture. If you make your own pasta, it is worth your while to search out this type of flour, at least for pasta salads. Use extra-virgin olive oil and make sure that your salad oil smells and tastes fresh. Fresh herbs aren't always available, so we use dried herbs in the recipes unless otherwise indicated.

Don't shy away from recipes that call for sesame paste, sesame oil or Chinese hot oil — these ingredients are now widely found in the import sections of large supermarkets, and will last indefinitely if refrigerated.

A word on substitutions: Feel free to use one vegetable in place of another, but keep in mind that the character of the dish may change, especially when only one or two vegetables are used. With pasta, the important thing is keeping the shapes similar — any long, thin pasta can be used in recipes calling for linguine, for example, just as shells could be substituted for, say, wagonwheel pasta.

Cook pasta only until al dente — meaning cooked through but still firm to the bite. Start testing packaged pasta after 5 minutes or so. The instant the pasta reaches the al dente stage, quickly drain it. Most fresh pasta cooks in mere minutes.

If the pasta is to be mixed with a dressing or sauce well in advance of serving, reserve a little. Since pasta tends to absorb liquid, you may want to add a little more dressing just before serving.

Chilling tends to decrease the intensity of some flavors and the recipes in this book take this effect into account. You may still want to taste a chilled salad just before serving and adjust seasonings to your own taste.

Presentation is important too. Clear salad bowls show off layered salads. Pasta salads heaped on serving platters invite attractive garnishes. Soup tureens, baskets lined with foil, trays and casseroles all make attractive serving pieces for pasta salads.

Contents

Pasta Salads with Seafood

Pasta Salads with Poultry

Pasta Salads with Meat

Dressings

Index

Pasta Salads with Vegetables

Pasta Salads with Vegetables

"*E*at your vegetables" — and now your parents' admonition is backed up by stacks of nutrition studies. Vegetables are high in vital nutrients and fiber, low in fat and calories. Combined with pasta they are pleasing mixtures of color and texture.

If calorie reduction is your goal, reduce the amount of pasta called for and increase the vegetables. When preparing salads, remember both vinegar and lemon juice in dressings will turn green vegetables an olive color. To keep the vegetables bright and fresh-looking, toss the pasta with part of the dressing to allow the flavor to be absorbed; add the vegetables and the rest of the dressing at the last minute.

To blanch vegetables, plunge them into a large quantity of boiling water for a minute or two, then immediately rinse with cold water to set the color and to maintain a crisp texture.

Pasta Capri

A real crowd-pleaser. A "do-ahead" warm weather menu could include cold poached chicken breasts napped with tarragon aspic, toasted pita bread spritzed with olive oil spray and sprinkled with herbs, and for dessert, cold pear halves poached in raspberry vinegar syrup.

8 ounces penne or small rigatoni
5 large tomatoes
4 cloves garlic, minced
25 leaves of fresh basil, torn into large pieces
3 long sweet yellow peppers or 2 green peppers
4 ounces low-fat mozzarella cheese, finely diced
2 tablespoons freshly grated Parmesan cheese

Dressing
¼ cup olive oil
1½ teaspoons salt
½ teaspoon freshly ground pepper

At least 2 hours before serving, slice the tomatoes, then slice again into strips. Seed peppers and cut into thin rounds if using long yellow peppers or into thin strips if using green peppers.

In a small bowl mix the tomatoes, peppers, garlic, basil leaves, oil, salt and pepper. Let stand without refrigerating.

Just before serving, cook pasta until al dente, drain well and put into a large shallow bowl. Add the mozzarella and the tomato mixture, sprinkle with grated Parmesan, toss and serve immediately.

Serves 6.

Hot Spaghetti with Cold Vegetable Sauce

A *simple and quickly made salad that is especially good with grilled chicken or fish, such as swordfish chunks marinated in lemon juice and thyme.*

12 ounces spaghetti or linguine
3 cups coarsely chopped fresh tomatoes
1½ cups peeled and seeded cucumber, cubed
2 cloves garlic, quartered
½ teaspoon oregano
½ teaspoon basil
Salt and pepper to taste
Tabasco sauce, if desired, to taste (about ½ teaspoon)

Cook pasta until al dente and drain well; keep hot.

While pasta is cooking, whirl rest of ingredients, including Tabasco if desired, in food processor or blender until almost smooth — leaving some of the vegetables in tiny pieces. Adjust seasonings to taste.

Toss sauce with hot spaghetti and serve.

Serves 6.

Spaghetti with Fresh Tomatoes and Mozzarella

*L*ook *for fresh low-fat mozzarella at Italian delis and gourmet shops.*

1 pound spaghetti
6 ripe tomatoes, cut into small cubes
4 ounces low-fat mozzarella, cut into small cubes
30 fresh basil leaves torn into quarters
$\frac{1}{4}$ cup olive or canola oil
Salt and pepper to taste
$\frac{1}{4}$ cup vegetable broth

Cook spaghetti to al dente stage and drain well. Toss while hot with remaining ingredients. Serve while still warm.

Serves 6.

Angel Hair with Tomato and Basil Sauce

*S*ubtle flavor in the sauce lifts a simple pasta dish to "angelic" heights.

12 ounces capellini or angel hair pasta
1 pound fresh plum tomatoes
1/4 cup fresh basil leaves, coarsely chopped
31/4-ounce jar capers, rinsed and drained
3 tablespoons sherry vinegar, or 2 tablespoons vinegar and 1 tablespoon sherry
1/2 teaspoon salt
1/2 teaspoon freshly ground pepper
1/4 cup olive or canola oil

Peel, seed and chop tomatoes. (Do not use a food processor.)

Combine with chopped basil and refrigerate overnight or prepare a few hours before serving but do not refrigerate.

Two hours before serving add the vinegar (or sherry and vinegar combination), capers and salt and pepper. Do not refrigerate.

Just before serving time add pasta to boiling, salted water and cook barely 4 minutes. Drain well and transfer to a rimmed platter or shallow bowl and toss with the oil. Add the tomato and basil sauce and serve.

Serves 6.

Gnocchi with Tart Tomato Sauce

*A*nother variation of a cold tomato sauce to make early before the heat of the summer day sets in. A frosted bowl of chilled spiced shrimp would accompany it well.

12 ounces dried gnocchi, conchiglie or cavatelli, tomato-flavored if possible though plain will do nicely
2 pounds garden-ripe tomatoes, seeded and roughly chopped
4 cloves garlic, minced
$\frac{1}{4}$ cup lemon juice
Grated rind of lemon
$1\frac{1}{2}$ teaspoons salt
$\frac{1}{2}$ teaspoon freshly ground black pepper
$\frac{1}{4}$ cup olive oil
$\frac{1}{4}$ cup tomato juice
$\frac{1}{4}$ cup basil vinegar
$\frac{1}{2}$ teaspoon sugar
$\frac{1}{4}$ cup finely chopped basil leaves
$\frac{1}{4}$ cup finely chopped parsley
Freshly grated Parmesan cheese

In a large serving bowl marinate chopped tomatoes, garlic, lemon juice and rind, salt, pepper, olive oil, tomato juice, vinegar and sugar. This mixture can marinate any number of hours, but do not refrigerate.

About 1 hour before serving cook pasta until al dente, drain, rinse with cold water and drain again. Add the chopped basil and parsley to the tomato marinade.

At serving time add the pasta to the tomato mixture and toss to coat the pasta.

Pass the Parmesan cheese separately.

Serves 6.

Spaghetti and Mozzarella Salad

*P*asta with a creamy texture and a tangy taste. This is a nice side dish with any broiled or poached fish or poultry or grilled flank steak, all very low in fat.

12 ounces spaghetti or fusilli
4 ounces low-fat mozzarella cheese, shredded
3 tomatoes, chopped
½ cup watercress, chopped
½ pound fresh snow peas, blanched, or ½ box frozen snow peas, thawed only
½ box frozen tiny green peas, thawed only
2 cloves garlic, minced
1 teaspoon salt
½ teaspoon freshly ground pepper

Dressing
4 tablespoons olive or canola oil
3 tablespoons herb vinegar
½ teaspoon sugar

Cook spaghetti until al dente, drain, rinse with cold water and drain again.

Add the shredded cheese to the hot pasta and stir over very low heat until cheese melts. (Don't worry if cheese seems gummy — it will separate when the other ingredients are added.) Remove from heat and toss gently with the remaining ingredients. Add dressing and toss again.

Serve at room temperature.

Serves 6.

Vermicelli in Tomato Shells

A *perfect first course in the summer when tomatoes and basil are at their peak. When tomatoes are out of season, serve the vermicelli by itself. And when fresh basil is lacking, try one of the pesto-type sauces on pages 167-170.*

8 ounces vermicelli
6 ripe tomatoes
½ cup pesto sauce
1 tablespoon pine nuts (or chopped walnuts)
Fresh basil leaves for garnish (optional)
Salt and pepper to taste

Pesto Sauce
2 cups fresh basil leaves
3 cloves garlic
½ cup grated Parmesan and Romano cheese, mixed
⅓ cup olive or canola oil

Hollow out tomatoes and drain well upside down. (Reserve tomato pulp for a cooked sauce, if desired.)

Cook vermicelli to al dente stage, drain, rinse with cold water and drain again.

While pasta is cooking, make pesto sauce by whirling sauce ingredients in the blender until smooth.

Toss vermicelli and pine nuts with pesto sauce, season to taste with salt and pepper. Fill tomatoes with pasta and garnish with optional basil leaves.

Serves 6.

Onions Oriental and Vermicelli

*A*n *unusual side dish or first course that will give your guests a pleasant surprise with its unexpected blend of spices in a pasta salad.*

12 ounces vermicelli
2 dozen small white onions — the smaller the better (Try the frozen ones.)
1/4 cup chopped parsley
2 tablespoons pine nuts
1/2 teaspoon freshly ground pepper

Dressing
1/4 cup olive or canola oil
2 teaspoons curry powder, or more to taste
1 teaspoon ground coriander
1/2 teaspoon ground cardamom or seeds from 4 cardamom pods
1/4 teaspoon turmeric
2 cloves garlic, minced
1 teaspoon salt
1 cup beef or chicken broth
1/2 cup white raisins

Cook vermicelli until al dente, drain, rinse under cold water and drain again. Transfer to a serving bowl; do not refrigerate.

Parboil peeled onions for 5 minutes in boiling, salted water, or slip peels off after boiling. If using frozen onions, simply thaw.

In medium-sized saucepan heat the oil, then add curry powder, coriander, cardamom and turmeric. Heat spices for a few minutes until fragrance is released. Add garlic, then parboiled onions, salt and broth. Boil uncovered for about 5 minutes, stirring occasionally. Remove the onions with a slotted spoon and add the raisins to the cooking liquid. Cook for 5 more minutes, then pour liquid over the onions. Add the parsley, pine nuts and ground pepper and let stand at room temperature for a few hours before serving.

At serving time add to the pasta and toss gently.

Serves 6.

Asian Primavera and Vermicelli

This salad would be a fitting accompaniment to any number of Asian main dishes such as crispy soy-marinated chicken, gingered shrimp and scallops on skewers, or beef with chili peppers.

12 ounces vermicelli
1 pound green beans, trimmed and cut in half
1 cup cauliflower, broken into bite-size florets
1 cup thinly sliced zucchini
½ cup thinly sliced red radishes
2 tablespoons toasted sesame seeds for garnish

Dressing
⅓ cup olive or canola oil
1 tablespoon sesame oil
1 tablespoon minced garlic
¼ cup soy sauce
¼ cup white wine vinegar
3 tablespoons dry sherry
1 teaspoon sugar
½ teaspoon salt

Cook vermicelli until al dente, drain, rinse with cold water and drain again.

Bring a pot of salted water to boil. Add cauliflower and blanch 1 minute. Remove with a slotted spoon and rinse under cold water. Drain and set aside to cool. Add beans to the boiling water and blanch for 2 minutes. Remove and rinse under cold water and cool completely.

Heat oil in small frying pan over medium heat. Saute garlic until barely golden. Remove pan from heat and add soy sauce, vinegar, sherry, sugar and salt.

Arrange vermicelli on a serving platter and add cauliflower, beans, zucchini and radishes in an attractive pattern. Drizzle dressing on top and sprinkle with sesame seeds. Toss at the table before serving.

Serves 6.

Fettuccine and Feta

This salad hints of the Greek Isles and is a fine beginning or side dish for a dinner that includes chicken roasted with garlic and oregano.

12 ounces fettuccine, fresh if available
3 ounces feta cheese, coarsely crumbled
½ box frozen snow peas, thawed only, or ¼ pound fresh, blanched and drained
¼ pound black Greek olives
1 green, red or yellow pepper, cut in strips
½ box cherry tomatoes, cut in half if large
¼ cup chopped walnuts

Dressing
¼ cup olive or canola oil
¼ cup vegetable broth
4 tablespoons red wine vinegar
½ teaspoon oregano
½ teaspoon dried mint, crushed
Salt and pepper to taste

Cook fettuccine until al dente, drain, rinse with cold water, and drain again. Combine with cheese, vegetables, and walnuts.

Shake olive oil, broth, vinegar, oregano, mint and salt and pepper in small jar until well combined; pour a quarter cup of the dressing at a time over the salad, mixing well after each addition — you may need less than the entire amount. Adjust seasonings. Serve at room temperature.

Serves 6.

Spinach and Rotelle Salad

*T*his healthful salad makes a nice substitute for the usual rice or potato side dish.

12 ounces rotelle
1 pound fresh spinach, thoroughly rinsed and tough stems removed
⅓ cup olive or canola oil
4 anchovy fillets, chopped into small pieces
2 cloves garlic, minced
⅓ cup parsley, minced
1 tablespoon pine nuts
Salt and pepper to taste

Cook pasta until al dente, drain, rinse with cold water and drain again. Do not refrigerate.

Stack spinach leaves, then slice crosswise into quarter-inch strips.

In a large frying pan, saute the anchovy fillets, garlic and pine nuts in oil until garlic and nuts are very lightly browned. Add spinach slices to the mixture and stir-fry until spinach is just wilted. Add contents of pan and the parsley to the rotelle, toss well, and add salt and pepper to taste. Serve at room temperature or slightly warm.

Serves 6.

Vegetable and Rotini Salad

Arrange the ingredients in layers in a large glass salad bowl and bring to the table so everyone can admire your salad before you toss it.

8 ounces rotini
½ bunch broccoli, stems peeled
1 teaspoon dried tarragon leaves, crushed
½ package frozen snow peas, thawed only (or 6 ounces fresh snow peas, quickly
    blanched and drained)
8 ounces fresh green beans, sliced on the diagonal and quickly cooked until crisp-tender
4 carrots, cut in julienne strips 2 inches long
1 tablespoon fresh chives, snipped, or 1 teaspoon dried
4 scallions, cut into thin rounds, including green part
½ box cherry tomatoes, cut in half if large
¼ cup chopped walnuts

Dressing
⅓ cup olive or canola oil
¼ cup fresh lemon juice
¼ teaspoon dry mustard, or 1 teaspoon prepared Dijon mustard
Salt to taste (start with ½ teaspoon)

Cook rotini until al dente, drain, rinse with cold water and drain again.

Cook broccoli in boiling salted water until crisp-tender. Drain and cool. Cut off florets; thinly slice stems.

In large glass serving bowl, layer the broccoli sprinkled with the tarragon, the julienned carrots sprinkled with the chives, half the pasta, the green beans sprinkled with the scallions, the rest of the pasta, the cherry tomatoes, the snow peas, and the walnuts. Cover and chill.

Combine the dressing ingredients and blend well. Pour over salad. Bring salad to table and toss.

Serves 6.

Caesar's Pasta

_____
_____
_____

*R*ecognize this old favorite? We hope you will enjoy the updated approach.

12 ounces vermicelli
1 clove garlic, lightly crushed
1 cooked egg white, chopped
1 small bunch romaine lettuce, sliced narrowly crosswise
1 cup herb-flavored croutons
¼ cup grated Parmesan cheese

Dressing
¼ cup olive or canola oil
2-3 tablespoons lemon juice
½ tin anchovy fillets, lightly mashed (reserve other half)
1 teaspoon salt
½ teaspoon freshly ground pepper
¼ teaspoon sugar

Rub a deep serving bowl with the crushed garlic clove.

Cook the vermicelli until al dente, drain, rinse with cold water and drain thoroughly. Add to the bowl and toss with the chopped egg white.

Blend dressing ingredients in a small bowl.

Add dressing, lettuce and Parmesan and toss.

Top with croutons, reserved anchovies and toss lightly just before serving.

Serves 6.

Twists and Eggplant

A favorite of an eggplant "freak" we know. Hearty enough to use as a main course but equally suitable for a first course. Makes a great leftover so don't worry about cutting back on amounts.

8 ounces small twist pasta or shells
1 large eggplant, peeled and diced
2 cups fresh or canned Italian plum tomatoes, chopped (save juice)
1 medium onion, chopped
1 cup celery, finely chopped
2 tablespoons minced parsley
1 clove garlic, minced
2 tablespoons olive oil, divided
1 teaspoon oregano
½ teaspoon thyme
Salt and freshly ground pepper to taste
3 tablespoons freshly grated Parmesan cheese

Place the peeled and diced eggplant in a colander, sprinkle with salt and let sit for about 30 minutes.

Cook pasta until al dente, drain, rinse with cold water and drain again. Transfer to a large serving bowl and set aside until sauce is ready.

Heat a non-stick skillet with ½ tablespoon olive oil. Saute celery for about 5 minutes. Add onion, parsley, garlic, oregano and thyme. Cook 5 minutes more and remove with a slotted spoon.

Rinse eggplant and pat dry with a paper towel. Heat skillet with ½ tablespoon oil and cook eggplant until soft. Combine all the cooked vegetables and add the tomatoes with their juice and the remaining tablespoon of oil. Bring to a boil, reduce heat, and cook at a low simmer for about ½ hour. Taste for seasonings. Cool slightly, then add to pasta; toss thoroughly with the Parmesan. Serve at room temperature.

Serves 6.

Eggplant and Linguine Salad

*H*ere's a simple treatment for eggplant. If you want to be fancy about it, add 2 tablespoons of pine nuts to the eggplant during the last minute or two of cooking and brown lightly.

12 ounces linguine
1 eggplant, about 1 pound
2 tablespoons capers, rinsed and drained
3 cloves garlic, lightly crushed
¼ cup olive oil
Salt and pepper to taste

Cook pasta until al dente, drain, rinse with cold water and drain again. Set aside.

Cut eggplant in half lengthwise and sprinkle heavily with salt; let stand ½ hour. (If eggplant is very young and fresh, this step can be omitted.) Rinse and dry eggplant, and cut into half-inch cubes.

In a large frying pan, saute the garlic in olive oil until lightly browned; discard garlic. Saute the cubed eggplant in the flavored oil over moderately high heat until browned, tossing and stirring.

Toss the eggplant, capers and salt and pepper with the pasta. Let sit at least ½ hour so flavors can blend. Adjust seasonings before serving.

Serves 6.

Vegetables Vinaigrette with Rotelle

A *"good anytime" salad since the vegetables are available year round. Remember, you can reduce the number of calories by proportionately increasing the vegetables and decreasing the pasta.*

8 ounces rotelle or any twist-type pasta
½ cauliflower
2 stalks broccoli
1 large carrot
½ pound green beans

Vinaigrette Dressing
¼ cup olive or canola oil
1 tablespoon red wine vinegar
1 teaspoon Dijon mustard
½ cup chopped red onion
2 tablespoons chopped parsley
½ teaspoon dried basil, crushed

Break cauliflower into florets and cook in boiled salted water barely 4 minutes. Drain, run under cold water and drain again.

Slice carrot into ½-inch rounds and cook 5 minutes in boiling salted water. Drain, run under cold water, and drain again.

Break broccoli into florets (save stems for another use) and cook in boiling salted water barely 2 minutes. Drain, rinse with cold water and drain again.

Whisk dressing ingredients until well blended. Combine vegetables and toss gently with the dressing. Refrigerate until ½ hour before serving.

Cook pasta until al dente, drain, rinse with cold water and drain again. Transfer to a large serving bowl and cool to room temperature.

Toss pasta with marinated vegetables ½ hour before serving; do not refrigerate again.

Serves 6.

Winter Pasta Salad

We call this a winter salad because the jarred vegetables it uses are sure to be available then. But because broccoli is available year-round, you can make it at any season you choose.

8 ounces pasta twists
1 pound broccoli florets, lightly cooked until crisp-tender (about 3 minutes)
Approximately 9 ounces pickled Italian vegetables (giardinera), drained
1 small jar sliced pimentos, drained

Dressing
¼ cup olive or canola oil
3 tablespoons wine vinegar
2 tablespoons vegetable broth
1 clove garlic, minced
1 teaspoon Dijon mustard
Salt and pepper to taste
½ teaspoon sugar

Cook twists until al dente, drain, rinse with cold water and drain again. Mix twists with broccoli, pickled vegetables and pimentos.

To make dressing, mix together vinegar, broth, garlic, and mustard. In blender or by hand using a whisk, slowly blend in oil, mixing well after each addition. Add salt and pepper to taste. Dressing should be fairly tart.

Add dressing to pasta and vegetable mixture, toss well, let stand at room temperature several hours so flavors can blend.

Serves 6.

A Pasta Salad with Character

This salad calls for a crunchy loaf of bread, a hearty jug of wine or lemonade, and at least six "thous" to share it.

12 ounces penne or elbow macaroni
½ box cherry tomatoes, halved
½ cup chopped parsley
½ cup cured black olives, Italian or Greek type
1 small red onion, thinly sliced

Dressing
¼ cup olive or canola oil
¼ cup vegetable broth
¼ cup tarragon or basil vinegar
1 teaspoon dried oregano, crushed
½ teaspoon dried basil or eight fresh basil leaves, chopped
¼ teaspoon dried red pepper flakes
4 cloves garlic, minced
¼ cup capers, rinsed and drained
1 tin anchovy fillets, drained and chopped

Cook pasta until al dente and drain well. Cool slightly in colander.

While pasta is cooking, mix dressing ingredients in a small bowl.

Transfer pasta to a serving bowl and toss with about ¼ cup dressing. Refrigerate if making early in the day but bring to room temperature before serving time. Add tomatoes, parsley, black olives, onions and remaining dressing to pasta. Toss gently before serving and taste for seasoning.

Serves 6.

Pickled Shells

*F*or the pickle lovers in your family, this nicely old-fashioned salad is sure to please.

8 ounces pasta shells
½ cup fat-free plain yogurt
¼ cup low-fat mayonnaise
1 tablespoon chopped onion
2 tablespoons chopped pimento
2 tablespoons chopped parsley
¼ teaspoon minced garlic
⅓ cup dill pickles, diced
1 tablespoon dill pickle juice, or as needed

Cook pasta shells until al dente, drain, rinse with cold water and drain again. Toss with remaining ingredients, using the pickle juice as necessary to get the right consistency. Chill at least two hours.

Serves 6.

Low-Salt Pasta Salad (with Variations)

*Y*ou *don't have to be on a special diet to enjoy this salad. With the addition of chicken or fish, it makes a satisfying and delicious main course. And you can vary the vegetables to suit what you have on hand.*

8 ounces rotini or medium pasta shells
2 tomatoes, diced
4 scallions, thinly sliced
1 cucumber, peeled, seeded, and diced
1 small red onion, diced
1/2 Spanish onion, diced
2 green and/or red peppers, seeded and diced
4 red potatoes, cooked and diced (do not peel)
1 bunch broccoli, briefly cooked and diced
1/2 pound green beans, briefly cooked and diced
1/4 cup parsley, minced
Fresh basil to taste, if available

Dressing
1/4 cup rice vinegar
1/2 teaspoon Dijon mustard
Pinch oregano
1/2 teaspoon pepper
1 tablespoon frozen apple juice

Variations
1 pound boned and skinned chicken breasts, poached (covered) with 2 teaspoons dried
    basil leaves, then cooled and diced
OR
1 pound salmon, sole or halibut fillet, poached with 1 teaspoon dried thyme, cooled and
    flaked

Cook pasta until al dente, drain, rinse with cold water and drain again. Toss pasta with the vegetables (and chicken or fish, if desired).

Shake dressing ingredients in covered jar until well blended, pour over other ingredients, and toss again. Serve at room temperature or lightly chilled.

Serves 6.

White Kidney Bean and Macaroni Salad

This hearty salad could be a meal by itself. Or serve it with sliced turkey and good rye bread for an easy meal after the big game.

8 ounces macaroni
1 20-ounce can white kidney beans, rinsed and drained
1 cup diced mixed green and red pepper
1/4 cup minced fresh parsley
2 cloves garlic, minced
1 box small cherry tomatoes
1/3 cup vegetable broth
2 tablespoons olive or canola oil
4 tablespoons white wine vinegar
Salt and pepper to taste

Cook macaroni until al dente, drain, rinse with cold water and drain again. Add vegetables and toss.

In small bowl whisk broth, oil, vinegar and salt and pepper together, pour over macaroni and vegetable mixture and toss thoroughly. Let stand so flavors can blend. Serve at room temperature or slightly chilled.

Serves 6.

Pasta Salad Nicoise

All the wonderful flavor of the classic Nicoise salad but simpler to construct. Make early in the day or the day before to let the flavors "marry."

8 ounces rotelle, wheels or shell pasta
2 egg whites, diced
2 tomatoes, diced
1 tin anchovies, drained and chopped
1/4 cup capers, rinsed and drained
1/2 cup cured black olives, sliced
2 small red onions, coarsely chopped
2 canned pimentos, sliced
1/2 cup chopped parsley

Dressing
3 tablespoons basil vinegar or white wine vinegar
1/3 cup olive or canola oil
2 cloves garlic, minced
1 teaspoon salt or to taste
1/2 teaspoon freshly ground pepper

Cook pasta until al dente, drain, rinse with cold water and drain again. Set aside.

In a small bowl whisk together all dressing ingredients.

In a deep serving bowl put a layer of half the pasta, then a layer of half of the eggs, tomatoes, anchovies, capers, olives, onions, pimentos and 1/4 cup parsley.

Sprinkle with half of the dressing.

Make a second layer of pasta, remaining half of the ingredients and sprinkle with the remaining dressing. Refrigerate until 1/2 hour before serving time. Toss very slightly before serving.

Serves 6.

Tomatoes Nicoise and Linguine

A *simple and simply delicious side dish. The perky dressing will even pep up winter tomatoes, but summer ones are best.*

12 ounces linguine
3 tomatoes, peeled and thinly sliced
12 Italian black olives
3 tablespoons freshly grated Parmesan cheese
¼ cup chopped parsley

Dressing
¼ cup olive or canola oil
2 tablespoons red wine vinegar
4 anchovy fillets, patted dry and chopped
2 cloves garlic, minced
¼ teaspoon freshly ground pepper
Salt to taste

Cook pasta until al dente, drain, rinse with cold water and drain again.

Mix all dressing ingredients in a medium bowl. Add the tomatoes and black olives. Marinate at room temperature at least 1 hour.

Mix the Parmesan cheese and chopped parsley and set aside. At serving time add the tomato mixture to the pasta and toss. Sprinkle with the cheese and parsley mixture and divide among 6 salad plates or bowls.

Serves 6.

Fettuccine and Tomatoes with Lemon Dressing

*T*his fresh-tasting salad will sharpen jaded summer appetites. To keep the lemon theme going, serve the salad with chicken pieces marinated in lemon and herbs and grilled on the barbecue.

1 pound fettuccine, fresh if desired
4-6 ripe tomatoes, diced
6-8 basil leaves, roughly torn
Juice of 1 lemon
4 tablespoons olive or canola oil
Salt and pepper to taste

Cook fettuccine to the al dente stage and drain well. Toss immediately with the oil, lemon juice, and salt and pepper to taste. Toss again with the tomatoes and basil. Adjust seasonings and serve warm or at room temperature.

Serves 6.

Garden Fresh Pasta Salad

A melange of the freshest summer vegetables and a simple-to-make pesto sauce result in an easy and vitamin-packed main dish.

8 ounces rigatoni or other large tube pasta
Sliced and cubed fresh vegetables to equal 4 cups: green beans, zucchini, yellow squash,
 eggplant, red or green peppers
2 cups packed fresh basil leaves
¼ cup vegetable broth
¼ cup olive or canola oil, divided
2 tablespoons pine nuts or coarsely chopped walnuts
3 cloves garlic, minced
1 teaspoon salt
½ teaspoon freshly ground pepper
¼ cup freshly grated Parmesan cheese
12 cherry tomatoes, halved if large

Put the basil leaves, broth, 3 tablespoons oil and salt into a blender or food processor and blend just until combined but not pureed. In a small skillet heat the 1 tablespoon oil and lightly brown the pine nuts. Add the garlic and let it barely color.

Cook the pasta until al dente and drain. Transfer to a serving bowl and toss with the oil, garlic, pine nuts and freshly ground pepper.

In a large pot of boiling salted water cook the beans about 3 minutes, add the squash and eggplant and cook an additional 2 minutes. Drain and plunge into cold water to stop the cooking and retain the color. Drain thoroughly.

Add cooked vegetables to the pasta along with the pesto sauce and toss gently. Add the cheese and cherry tomatoes and toss again. Serve at room temperature.

Serves 6.

Vegetable and Pasta Salad with Pizazz

Spice up an otherwise ordinary meal with a side dish of snappy salad served at room temperature. It's equally good summer or winter.

12 ounces fettuccine
3 cups chopped broccoli, cooked 2 minutes until crisp
1/2 pint cherry tomatoes, halved
1/4 cup olive or canola oil
3 cloves garlic, minced
1/2 cup chopped onions
2 tablespoons fresh basil, chopped, or 2 teaspoons dried basil, crushed
1/4 teaspoon red pepper flakes, or more to taste
1 teaspoon salt
1/2 teaspoon freshly ground pepper
2 tablespoons freshly grated Parmesan cheese

Cook fettuccine until al dente, drain, rinse with cold water and drain again. In a serving bowl, toss pasta with cheese.

Heat 1/4 cup oil in a large skillet and saute onions until tender. Add garlic and basil and cook briefly. Add tomatoes, cook about 2 minutes, then sprinkle with the salt and pepper.

Remove pan from heat and cool mixture a bit. Very gently stir in the cooked broccoli and red pepper flakes. Add to the pasta and cheese and toss at the table.

Serves 6.

Roasted Pepper, Zucchini and Pasta Salad

A *year-round salad. The jarred roast peppers are a tasty substitute for the fresh variety. The bright green and red colors would be an appealing addition to a Christmas buffet table.*

8 ounces rotelle or penne
3 medium zucchini
3 red peppers, roasted, or a 7-ounce jar roasted peppers, drained
5 cloves garlic, minced
2 tablespoons olive oil
1/4 cup vegetable broth
1 1/2 teaspoons oregano, crushed
3 tablespoons chopped parsley
1 teaspoon salt, divided
1/2 teaspoon freshly ground pepper
2 tablespoons white wine vinegar

Cook the pasta until al dente, drain, rinse with cold water and drain again. Transfer to a large bowl.

Halve the zucchini lengthwise and slice into 1/4-inch pieces. Salt lightly and let drain for 30 minutes. Pat dry.

Meanwhile, if using fresh red peppers, roast them under a preheated broiler until all sides are charred. Wrap in foil or close up in a brown paper bag. When cool, slip off charred skins, remove seeds and cut in narrow strips. Cut drained, jarred peppers into narrow strips.

Heat oil in a large skillet and saute the zucchini for no more than 2 minutes. Remove with a slotted spoon to a bowl.

Add garlic to the skillet and cook over low heat about 1 minute or until the garlic lightly browns. Add the oregano and broth and heat briefly; pour mixture over the roasted peppers. Add the parsley, salt, pepper, and vinegar. Stir and add to the cooled pasta.

Toss lightly and place the zucchini on top but do not toss until ready to serve. This will prevent the zucchini from turning an off shade of green. Refrigerate until 30 minutes before serving time.

Serves 6.

Artichoke and Pasta Salad with Tomato Sauce

An easy side dish to accompany grilled rosemary chicken or broiled fish.

8 ounces ziti
1 6-ounce jar marinated artichoke hearts
1/2 cup chopped onions
2 cloves garlic, minced
2 cups peeled and diced tomatoes or 1 16-ounce can Italian plum tomatoes,
    drained and chopped
1 bay leaf
1 teaspoon salt
Freshly ground pepper to taste
1/2 teaspoon oregano, crushed
1/4 teaspoon marjoram, crushed
1/2 teaspoon basil, crushed, or 1 tablespoon fresh basil, chopped
2 tablespoons chopped parsley
2 tablespoons freshly grated Parmesan cheese

Cook pasta until al dente, drain, rinse with cold water and drain again.
Transfer to a serving bowl.

Drain marinade from the artichokes into a 10-inch skillet. Set the
artichokes aside. Add the garlic and onions to the liquid and simmer until
the onions become translucent. Add the tomatoes, bay leaf, herbs and
salt. Cover and simmer 10 minutes. Uncover and cook another 10
minutes. Cut the artichokes in half and add to the tomato sauce. Heat for
a few minutes. Remove the bay leaf and stir in the parsley. Cool to room
temperature and pour over the pasta. Toss with cheese until well
blended.

Serves 6.

Fettuccine and Mushroom Salad

*A*n almost traditional pasta first course, with a twist: this pasta in a low-fat creamy sauce is served cold.

12 ounces fettuccine
8 large mushrooms (about ¼ pound)
4 green onions
¼ cup grated Parmesan cheese
¼ cup minced parsley
½ cup low-fat or non-fat sour cream
2 tablespoons skim milk
2 tablespoons olive oil
3 tablespoons tarragon or basil vinegar
Salt and freshly ground pepper to taste
½ teaspoon crushed tarragon

Cook pasta until al dente, drain, rinse with cold water and drain again.

Thinly slice mushrooms and green onions and place in a large shallow serving bowl; add all remaining ingredients except the fettuccine. Mix thoroughly. Add the pasta but do not toss. Cover with plastic wrap and chill for several hours.

Bring to room temperature and toss before serving.

Taste for seasonings and divide among 6 salad plates.

Serves 6.

Broccoli Walnut Primavera

Primavera means "springtime" but this variation has year-round appeal. When fresh basil is not available for the dressing, substitute fresh spinach and dried basil.

12 ounces fettuccine
2 large ripe tomatoes, or 1 basket cherry tomatoes
1 bunch broccoli
$\frac{1}{2}$ cup pitted black olives, sliced
$\frac{1}{4}$ cup coarsely chopped walnuts

Dressing
1 cup fresh basil leaves (or 1 cup fresh spinach and 2 teaspoons dried basil)
$\frac{1}{4}$ cup olive or canola oil
2 cloves garlic
2 tablespoons grated Parmesan cheese
2 tablespoons red wine vinegar
$\frac{1}{2}$ teaspoon salt
$\frac{1}{4}$ teaspoon freshly ground pepper

Cook pasta until al dente, drain, rinse with cold water and drain again. Place in a large shallow bowl.

Seed tomatoes and chop coarsely, or halve cherry tomatoes. Slice peeled broccoli stems $\frac{1}{4}$ inch thick and break florets into smaller pieces. Cook broccoli 3 minutes in boiling salted water. Drain, rinse with cold water and drain again.

Add tomatoes, broccoli, olives and walnuts to the pasta and toss gently.

In a blender or food processor chop the basil (or spinach), garlic, walnuts, Parmesan cheese and vinegar. Add the olive oil in a slow stream until it is all absorbed. Stir in the salt and pepper.

Pour dressing over the salad and toss thoroughly but gently. Serve slightly chilled or at room temperature.

Serves 6.

Pasta Primavera, Again

There are endless versions of pasta primavera and we love them all; here is still another to enjoy.

12 ounces linguine or fettuccine
1 pound zucchini
½ bunch (about ½ pound) broccoli
½ pound green beans
3 tablespoons olive oil
6 shallots or 4 scallions, white part only
2 cloves garlic, minced
¼ cup chopped parsley
2 tablespoons fresh basil, chopped or 2 teaspoons dried basil, crushed
1 teaspoon salt
Freshly ground pepper
¼ cup vegetable broth
2 tablespoons freshly grated Parmesan cheese

Cook pasta until al dente, drain, rinse with cold water and drain again. Transfer to a shallow bowl.

Wash and trim all vegetables and chop into rather small pieces.

Heat oil in a large skillet that has a cover. Add the vegetables, and stir to coat with oil. Add the shallots and garlic. Cover and steam over high heat for 5 minutes. Uncover and add the basil and parsley and stir well. Cook slightly longer; the vegetables should be crunchy.

Season vegetables with the salt and pepper and add to the pasta. Toss well and let come to room temperature. Add up to ¼ cup of vegetable broth just before serving if salad seems dry.

Garnish with the Parmesan cheese.

Serves 6.

Crunchy, Curried Pasta Salad

*A*dd some zest to that simple sandwich meal you're planning after a hard day's work or a lazy day at the beach.

8 ounces shells, wheels or macaroni
1 green or red pepper, roughly chopped
1/2 cup sliced celery
6 green onions, cut into 1/2-inch slices
1 small jar pimentos, drained and chopped
1/4 cup chopped parsley

Dressing
1/4 cup low-fat mayonnaise
1/4 cup fat-free sour cream or fat-free yogurt
2 tablespoons olive oil
2 tablespoons vinegar
2 teaspoons curry powder
1 teaspoon salt
1/4 teaspoon pepper

Cook pasta until al dente, drain, rinse under cold water and drain again. Cover with plastic wrap and refrigerate. Prepare vegetables and blend dressing ingredients in a small bowl. Toss all vegetables and dressing with cold pasta and chill thoroughly. Let flavors blend for several hours if possible.

Serves 6.

Ultra-Simple Green Pasta Salad

*A*n almost instant side dish to serve with a variety of meat, poultry or seafood main dishes.

12 ounces green fettuccine
1 4-ounce jar whole pimentos, cut in strips
1/2 cup chopped green onions (including tops)
1/4 cup chopped parsley
1 tablespoon olive oil
1 tablespoon vinegar
1/4 teaspoon salt
1/8 teaspoon freshly ground pepper
1/2 teaspoon oregano, crushed
1/4 cup low-fat mayonnaise or fat-free yogurt
1/4 cup vegetable broth
1/2 teaspoon salt
1/4 teaspoon freshly ground pepper
1 tablespoon toasted sunflower seeds, optional

Cook fettuccine until al dente, drain, rinse with cold water and drain again. Transfer to a serving bowl and toss with the olive oil, vinegar, salt, pepper, oregano, pimentos, green onions and parsley.

Mix the mayonnaise or yogurt and broth and remaining salt and pepper together and add to the pasta with the sunflower seeds; toss again.

Serves 6.

Linguine Salad with Anchovies and Olives

This simple-seeming salad is really quite sophisticated in flavor. It's a wonderful start to a meal that's based on the flavors of the Mediterranean.

12 ounces linguine
18 cured black olives, pitted
1 tin flat anchovy fillets, drained
$\frac{1}{4}$ cup minced parsley
$\frac{1}{4}$ cup olive oil
Freshly ground black pepper

Cook pasta until al dente, drain, rinse with cold water and drain again.

Slice the pitted olives into thin strips. Chop the anchovies into small, firm pieces; do not mash.

Toss the pasta with the olive oil, olives and anchovies. Let sit for at least $\frac{1}{2}$ hour so flavors can blend. Just before serving, toss again with the parsley and freshly ground black pepper to taste.

Serves 6.

Sweet and Sour Orzo and Vegetable Salad

*T*his combination makes a refreshing first course or side dish with cold turkey sandwiches.

1½ cups orzo
1 cup seeded, peeled and chopped cucumber
1 cup chopped carrots
½ cup chopped green onions
Lettuce leaves

Dressing
½ cup white wine vinegar
2 tablespoons olive or canola oil
3 tablespoons sugar
1 tablespoon chopped fresh dill or 1 teaspoon dried dillweed
1 teaspoon salt
¼ teaspoon ground red pepper
1 tablespoon toasted sesame seeds for garnish

Cook pasta until al dente, drain, rinse with cold water and drain thoroughly. Refrigerate.

Prepare vegetables and dressing. Add to cold pasta and gently stir to mix. Cover and refrigerate until serving time, at least 1 hour.

Line a serving bowl with lettuce leaves and mound salad on top; sprinkle with sesame seeds. Or place lettuce and salad on individual salad plates and serve as a first course.

Serves 6.

Mystery Garden Pasta Salad

*T*his is easy and quick and fun to serve. Your family or guests will be hard-pressed to identify the mystery ingredient (wheat germ).

12 ounces linguine
$\frac{1}{2}$ pound broccoli
5 medium carrots
4 quarts boiling water
1 teaspoon salt
12 cherry tomatoes, halved
$\frac{1}{2}$ cup chopped green onions
1 tablespoon toasted sesame seeds

Dressing
$\frac{1}{4}$ cup wheat germ, whirled in a blender or processor until fine
$\frac{1}{3}$ cup olive or canola oil
1 teaspoon sesame oil
$\frac{1}{4}$ cup lemon juice
3 tablespoons soy sauce
2 cloves garlic

Add all the dressing ingredients to the wheat germ in blender or processor and process 30 seconds. Peel broccoli stems and slice $\frac{1}{4}$ inch thick. Break heads into small florets. Peel and thinly slice carrots. Break linguine into 3-inch pieces.

Add the linguine to the boiling, salted water and cook 3 minutes. Add broccoli and carrots and cook 3 minutes longer. Drain, rinse with cold water and drain thoroughly again. Transfer to a large serving bowl and toss gently with about $\frac{1}{2}$ cup dressing. Refrigerate.

Before serving add tomatoes, green onions and sesame seeds and drizzle with more dressing to taste.

Serves 6.

Sesame Pasta Salad

This pasta salad can be addictive. And it's so simple to make, you'll be able to satisfy your craving often.

12 ounces linguine
3 tablespoons Chinese sesame oil
4 tablespoons soy sauce
$\frac{1}{2}$ teaspoon minced garlic
$\frac{1}{2}$ cup minced watercress
$\frac{1}{2}$ red pepper, finely diced
1 teaspoon hot chili oil (or to taste)
Salt and freshly ground black pepper to taste

Cook linguine until al dente, drain well and toss with remaining ingredients. Chill salad for several hours and preferably overnight.

Serves 6.

Szechuan Dan Dan Noodles

*W*e are providing a number of sesame and noodle recipes to let you discover your favorite — as well as the one that calls for ingredients available in your area.

1 pound vermicelli or linguine

Dressing
¼ cup sesame seeds, toasted and crushed
½ cup scallions, minced, green included
2 cloves garlic, minced
2 tablespoons grated fresh ginger
1 tablespoon Chinese sesame oil
½ cup red wine vinegar
2 teaspoons sugar
1 teaspoon hot chili oil
1 teaspoon Szechuan peppercorns, crushed in a mortar, if available
½ cup cilantro (Chinese parsley), coarsely chopped

Cook the pasta until al dente, drain, rinse with cold water and drain again.

While pasta is cooking, mix the dressing ingredients together. Adjust the seasonings. You may want to add the hot chili oil and the pepper a little at a time until it suits your taste.

Immediately toss the pasta with the dressing; garnish with additional cilantro leaves and sliced scallion if desired. Serve at room temperature or chilled.

Serves 6.

Oriental Pasta Salad

*T*he complementary flavors of rich, nutty whole wheat pasta and crunchy
oriental vegetables make this unique salad a vegetarian delight. The
addition of protein-rich tofu makes it nutritious as well as delicious.

12 ounces whole wheat fusilli, fresh if possible
4 green onions, green part only, sliced
1 small bottle baby corn, drained
1 8-ounce can bamboo shoots, drained, rinsed and julienned
1 8-ounce can water chestnuts, drained, rinsed and sliced
1 cup shredded carrots
½ pound tofu, cubed (optional)
3 tablespoons sesame oil, divided
¼ cup soy sauce

Cook the pasta until al dente, drain, rinse with cold water and drain again.
Transfer to a large bowl and toss with 1 tablespoon sesame oil.

Mix the remaining sesame oil and the soy sauce in a small bowl.

Add the remaining ingredients to the pasta, pour the dressing over and
toss to coat thoroughly.

Serve at room temperature.

Serves 6.

Ginger and Scallion Lo Mein Salad

A good accompaniment for chicken or duck basted with a soy sauce marinade and roasted.

1 pound thin egg noodles, fresh if possible
1-inch portion fresh ginger, peeled and minced
1 bunch scallions, coarsely chopped
Olive oil spray
½ cup chicken broth
1 teaspoon sugar
2 tablespoons soy sauce
2 tablespoons hoisin sauce
2 tablespoons sesame oil

Cook noodles until al dente, drain, rinse with cold water, drain well. Toss with the sesame oil.

Stir-fry ginger and scallions in the oil-sprayed non-stick pan. Add rest of ingredients, mix well.

Toss noodles with the sauce mixture. Add a little more sesame oil if necessary. Let come to room temperature and serve.

Serves 6.

Simple Asian Noodle Salad

This salad is as uncluttered as a Japanese home and each flavor is distinct on the palate.

12 ounces rice sticks or capellini
2 tablespoons soy sauce
2 tablespoons chicken or vegetable broth
3 tablespoons sesame oil
1 tablespoon sesame-chili oil
4 tablespoons rice vinegar
Salt, to taste
1 tablespoon toasted sesame seeds
⅔ cup finely snipped chives or finely chopped green onion tops
⅓ cup finely chopped parsley

Cook pasta until al dente, drain thoroughly. Toss with the soy sauce, broth, sesame and sesame-chili oils and the rice vinegar. Cover with plastic wrap and chill for several hours or overnight.

Just before serving, add sesame seeds, chives and parsley and toss lightly. Adjust seasoning if necessary.

Serves 6.

Fettuccine in Walnut Sauce

A good first course. It looks especially nice served on a large platter surrounded by a vegetable salad of cherry tomatoes, sliced Jerusalem artichokes, and green pepper squares dressed in a low-fat vinaigrette.

12 ounces fettuccine
1 small bunch parsley, washed and stems removed
4 ounces shelled walnuts
3 cloves garlic, minced
$\frac{1}{4}$ cup olive or canola oil
$\frac{1}{4}$ cup vegetable broth
1 teaspoon salt
$\frac{1}{2}$ teaspoon freshly ground pepper

Cook fettuccine until al dente, drain, rinse with cold water and drain again.

In blender or food processor, whirl parsley, walnuts, garlic, and broth with the oil added in a slow stream. Add salt and pepper and blend again.

Toss fettuccine and $\frac{1}{2}$ cup walnut sauce. Chill to allow flavors to blend. Add more sauce if the pasta has absorbed too much of the sauce and is dry. May be served chilled or at room temperature.

Serves 6.

San Remo Pasta Salad

Quite elegant in its simplicity, this salad will be a perfect side dish for many grilled meat, fish and poultry entrees.

12 ounces fusilli
1/2 cup chopped oil-packed sun-dried tomatoes
1/2 cup chopped fresh basil
1/4 cup freshly grated Parmesan cheese
1/2 cup black Italian or Greek olives
Oil from dried tomatoes
2 tablespoons basil vinegar
1/2 teaspoon salt or more to taste
1/2 teaspoon freshly ground black pepper

Cook pasta until al dente, drain, rinse with cold water and drain again.

Add all remaining ingredients and toss lightly. Taste for seasoning and adjust to taste.

Serve at room temperature or lightly chilled.

Serves 6.

Tortellini Salad

*E*asy *to do because the tortellini can be purchased from an Italian grocery store or in the frozen-food section of most supermarkets. Check the Italian market for some fresh, crisp arugula for the salad and a crunchy bread to round out the meal.*

1 pound tortellini, vegetarian if available, or agnolotti
2 red peppers or 1 small jar whole pimentos
½ cup chopped green onions
¼ cup cured chopped black olives
2 tablespoons toasted chopped walnuts

Dressing
¼ cup olive or canola oil
3 tablespoons wine vinegar
⅓ cup vegetable or chicken broth, fat removed
2 teaspoons Dijon mustard
2 tablespoons chopped parsley
2 tablespoons chopped fresh dill or 1 teaspoon dried dillweed
1 tablespoon fresh oregano or 1 teaspoon dried oregano, crushed
1 teaspoon salt
¼ teaspoon freshly ground black pepper

Cook the pasta in boiling salted water, 5 to 10 minutes for fresh, 10 to 15 minutes for frozen. Test before draining. Drain, rinse with cold water and drain thoroughly.

Slice the peppers or pimentos into thin strips. Rinse the cured olives and drain. Mix all the dressing ingredients thoroughly.

In a large bowl carefully mix the pasta, peppers, onions, olives, walnuts and ⅓ cup of the dressing. Cover and chill a few hours.

Before serving taste for salt and pepper and add more dressing to taste.

Serves 6.

Agnolotti and Tomato Salad

*U*nfortunately, summer is really the only time to savor this salad. Fresh tomatoes and basil are absolutely essential to the finished product. It's worth waiting for.

1 pound agnolotti or tortellini, vegetarian if available
2 pounds small tomatoes, cut into thin wedges
4 ounces low-fat mozzarella, shredded
½ cup Italian cured black olives (or Nicoise if available)
¼ cup finely chopped parsley, for garnish

Dressing
3 tablespoons vegetable broth
¼ cup olive or canola oil
¼ cup white wine or basil vinegar
2 tablespoons minced fresh basil
1 teaspoon salt
Freshly ground pepper to taste (use a lot)

Cook the pasta in boiling salted water 5 to 10 minutes if fresh and 10 to 15 minutes if frozen; test before draining. Drain, rinse under cold water and drain again. Transfer to a large bowl.

Add the tomato wedges, mozzarella slices and olives to the pasta.

Beat the dressing ingredients together in a small bowl until well combined.

Drizzle dressing over the salad and toss gently. Serve at room temperature for maximum flavor but chilled is almost as good.

Serves 6.

Rotelle, Mushrooms and Broccoli with a Light Tomato Sauce

*H*ere *is a satisfying side dish to accompany any grilled or broiled entree: trimmed lamb chops, rosemary chicken or lemon-basted thick fish fillets, for example.*

8 ounces rotelle
1 pound mushrooms, quartered
1½ cups broccoli, coarsely chopped and blanched
2 tablespoons olive oil
¼ cup fat-free yogurt
1 cup canned plum tomatoes, drained and coarsely chopped
1 teaspoon oregano, crushed
1 teaspoon basil, crushed
½ teaspoon salt or more to taste
½ teaspoon freshly ground pepper, or to taste
2 teaspoons freshly grated Parmesan cheese

Cook pasta until al dente, drain, rinse with cold water and drain again.

Heat 2 tablespoons olive oil in a large skillet, add the mushrooms and saute quickly over high heat until golden.

Remove from heat and add yogurt, tomatoes, and seasonings. Mix well and cool to room temperature.

Toss the mushroom sauce with the pasta.

Add the broccoli just before serving and toss gently again. Taste for seasoning.

Serve at room temperature and sprinkle with the grated Parmesan.

Serves 6.

Shells, Peas and Banana Peppers

The yellow pepper rings and the fresh green peas add colorful — and tasty — accents to this simple salad.

8 ounces shell pasta
1 pound fresh peas, shelled and blanched
3 long yellow peppers, sliced in thin rings
2 ounces fontina cheese, shredded
2 cloves garlic, minced
¼ cup chopped parsley

Dressing
⅓ cup olive or canola oil
3 tablespoons basil vinegar
1 tablespoon fat-free yogurt
1 teaspoon basil, crushed, or 1 tablespoon minced fresh basil
½ teaspoon salt
½ teaspoon freshly ground black pepper

Cook pasta until al dente, drain, rinse with cold water and drain again.

Plunge shelled peas for about 1 minute into 1 quart boiling water. Drain and dry with paper toweling.

Add peas, sliced peppers, cheese and garlic to pasta in serving bowl. Add ⅓ cup dressing and toss; taste for seasoning. Add remaining dressing just before serving. Serve at room temperature or lightly chilled.

Serves 6.

Linguine with Artichoke, Basil and Walnut Sauce

*F*resh basil is a must for this salad but frozen artichoke hearts simplify the preparations.

12 ounces spinach linguine
1/4 cup olive oil
1 9-ounce package frozen artichoke hearts, thawed and quartered
4 cloves garlic, minced
1/4 cup coarsely chopped walnuts
1/2 cup fresh basil leaves minced
1/4 cup vegetable broth
1/2 cup chopped parsley
1 teaspoon oregano
1 teaspoon salt
1/2 teaspoon freshly ground black pepper

Cook the pasta until al dente, drain, rinse with cold water and drain again.

Heat oil and add artichoke hearts and saute until golden; add garlic and walnuts and saute until walnuts color slightly. Remove from heat.

Add the broth, basil, parsley, oregano, salt and pepper; mix well and let cool without refrigerating.

Toss with the pasta and serve at room temperature.

Serves 6.

Diet-Wise Pasta, Mushroom and Pepper Salad

The original recipe called for regular mayonnaise and creme fraiche! If you want to be really ascetic about it, use no-fat products.

12 ounces spinach tagliatelle
½ pound mushrooms, thinly sliced
2 green peppers, cored, seeded and thinly sliced
2 red peppers, cored, seeded and thinly sliced
¼ cup chopped parsley

Dressing
½ cup lemon juice, divided
½ cup low-fat mayonnaise
1 cup fat-free yogurt
¼ cup tarragon vinegar
1 tablespoon basil, crushed
2 teaspoons tarragon, crushed
1 teaspoon salt or more to taste
½ teaspoon freshly ground black pepper or more to taste

Marinate the mushrooms in ¼ cup lemon juice overnight.

Cook the pasta until al dente, drain, rinse under cold water and drain again.

Drain mushrooms and discard juice.

Combine mayonnaise, yogurt, mushrooms, vinegar, herbs, salt and pepper.

Add green and red pepper slices and parsley to pasta. Add half the dressing and mix gently but thoroughly. Cover with plastic wrap and chill at least 4 hours before serving. Add additional dressing to taste.

Serves 6.

Capellini with Broccoli and Goat Cheese

*H*ere is a first course that might be followed by quickly grilled fish fillets flavored with lemon and rosemary, small new potatoes rolled in crumbs and sauteed in a Pam-sprayed non-stick pan and a crisp salad of arugula with a mild vinaigrette dressing.

12 ounces capellini or vermicelli
1½ cups small broccoli florets
⅓ cup olive oil, divided
½ teaspoon thyme, crushed
1 clove garlic, minced
½ teaspoon salt
2 ounces goat cheese, cut into slivers or crumbled
Freshly ground black pepper

Cook the pasta until al dente, drain, rinse with cold water and drain again.

Heat the oil in a small skillet and add the broccoli florets, thyme, garlic and salt. Toss broccoli to coat in oil and heat briefly; it should remain crisp.

Remove from heat and toss with the pasta. Cool to room temperature.

Just before serving add goat cheese and freshly ground black pepper to taste. Divide among six salad plates.

Serves 6.

White, Green and Black Pasta Salad

*S*ophisticated *colors enhance this snappy salad.*

8 ounces rotelle or rotini
1 cup green beans, julienned in $1\frac{1}{2}$-inch lengths
$\frac{1}{2}$ cup zucchini, halved lengthwise and sliced across
$\frac{1}{2}$ cup chopped sweet pickles
$\frac{1}{4}$ cup chopped Bermuda onion
2 tablespoons capers, rinsed and drained
$\frac{1}{4}$ cup small pitted black olives

Dressing
$\frac{1}{4}$ cup low-fat mayonnaise
$\frac{1}{4}$ cup fat-free yogurt
2 tablespoons lemon juice
1 tablespoon olive oil
$\frac{1}{2}$ teaspoon salt
$\frac{1}{2}$ teaspoon freshly ground black pepper

Cook pasta until al dente, drain, rinse with cold water and drain again.

Blanch green beans for 2 minutes in boiling water, drain, rinse with cold water and drain again.

Mix dressing ingredients in a small bowl.

Add beans, zucchini, chopped pickles, onion, capers and black olives to pasta in a large serving bowl.

Add the dressing and mix gently but thoroughly. Taste for seasoning. Chill at least 2 hours before serving.

Serves 6.

Mostaciolli and Broccoli with Low-Fat Creamy Garlic Dressing

W̶hat could be simpler? Cook the pasta, blanch the broccoli and whirl the dressing ingredients in a blender. Then serve and enjoy.

8 ounces mostaciolli or penne
1 pound broccoli
1 recipe Low-Fat Creamy Garlic Dressing (page 166)

Cook pasta until al dente, drain, rinse with cold water and drain again. Mix with ¼ cup of the Low-Fat Creamy Garlic Dressing.

Discard heavy bottom stems of broccoli. Peel remaining stems and slice ¼ inch thick. Break florets of broccoli into smaller pieces. Blanch stems and florets about 2 minutes in boiling water. Drain, rinse with cold water and drain again. Pat dry with paper towels. Add to pasta in serving bowl and toss with ½ cup (or more) of the dressing.

Serve at room temperature or lightly chilled.

Serves 6.

Marinated Vegetables with Pasta

The ultimate dieter's treat that is very low in calories, filling and nutritious.

8 ounces rotelle
3 carrots, diced
1 large zucchini, diced
1 cup coarsely chopped cauliflower
$\frac{1}{4}$ cup diced green pepper
$\frac{1}{4}$ cup chopped green onions
4 radishes, sliced
12 to 15 cherry tomatoes, halved

Dressing
$\frac{2}{3}$ cup fat-free yogurt
$\frac{1}{4}$ cup dry white wine
2 cloves garlic, minced
1 teaspoon dry mustard
1 teaspoon oregano, crushed
$\frac{1}{2}$ teaspoon basil, crushed
Salt and pepper to taste

Cook the rotelle until al dente, drain, rinse with cold water and drain again. Cover and refrigerate.

Mix dressing ingredients in a small bowl. Prepare vegetables and mix with the dressing. Refrigerate several hours or overnight.

To serve, arrange the pasta in a shallow bowl and top with the vegetables; do not toss.

Serves 6.

Healthful Vegetable and Orzo Salad

Another dieter's delight — lots of color, texture and flavor but few calories.

1 cup orzo, ave maria or other tiny pasta
½ cup coarsely chopped green or red pepper
¼ cup chopped radishes
½ cup peeled, seeded and chopped cucumber
2 tablespoons chopped parsley

Dressing
½ cup fat-free yogurt
3 tablespoons cider vinegar
1 tablespoon lemon juice
½ package or ⅛ teaspoon powdered artificial sweetener or ½ teaspoon sugar
2 teaspoons curry powder

Cook pasta until al dente, drain, rinse with cold water and drain again. Add vegetables and mix well.

Mix dressing ingredients in a small bowl and add to the pasta and vegetables. Mix lightly.

Cover and refrigerate for at least 6 hours or overnight.

Serves 6.

Almost Classic Pasta Salad

*W*e *think you will enjoy this variation of the dependable macaroni salad recipe that we all seem to have in our files.*

8 ounces shell or wheel pasta
2 tablespoons lemon juice
1 tablespoon olive oil
¼ cup chopped green onions
1 cup chopped celery with leaves
½ cup chopped parsley
½ cup sliced pimento-stuffed olives
¼ cup chopped green pepper
2 whites of hard-cooked eggs, chopped
1 tablespoon sunflower seeds
¼ cup low-fat mayonnaise or fat-free yogurt
¼ cup low-fat sour cream
1 teaspoon salt
½ teaspoon freshly ground black pepper
1 tablespoon white vinegar

Cook pasta until al dente, drain, rinse with cold water and drain again. In a large serving bowl mix the lemon juice and olive oil. Add the pasta, toss and refrigerate, covered, at least 1 hour.

Mix the mayonnaise or yogurt, sour cream, vinegar and seasonings in a small bowl.

At serving time add the vegetables, egg whites and sunflower seeds to the pasta. Add the dressing and mix thoroughly. Taste for seasoning.

Serves 6.

Pasta Salad Bar

A *wonderful idea for a buffet: Let your guests create their own pasta salad using their favorite ingredients. Provide plates or shallow bowls large enough to allow mixing. Set up the buffet table with a large bowl of pasta tossed with olive oil and smaller bowls containing other ingredients and pitchers of sauces and dressings. Below are some suggestions; amounts aren't given — that will depend on the number of guests and their appetites. Interesting breads, a choice of red or white wine or fruit juice spritzers, and dessert of fresh fruit salad and sherbet will complete the meal.*

Pasta
Twists, shells or ribbon-type pasta broken into shorter lengths for easier handling, cooked al dente, drained well and tossed with 1 tablespoon olive oil for each pound of pasta

Toppings
Scallions, chopped
Garlic, minced
Parsley, minced
Capers, rinsed and drained
Green olives
Black olives
Low-fat mozzarella or other low-fat mild cheese, julienned or grated
Parmesan cheese, grated
Feta cheese, crumbled
Green or red sweet peppers, julienned
Broccoli florets, blanched
Green beans, halved and blanched
Cucumbers, peeled, seeded, and diced
Cherry tomatoes, halved
Chick peas (garbanzo beans), rinsed and drained
Low-fat pepperoni or salami, julienned
Roast beef, julienned
Chicken breast, poached and shredded
Tuna fish, drained and chunked
Shellfish, such as shrimp, lobster or scallops, cooked and cut into small pieces
Flat anchovies, cut into tiny pieces

Dressings
Low-Fat Creamy Garlic Dressing (page 166)
Low-Fat Parsley Pesto (page 167)
Low-Fat Sesame Seed Vinaigrette (page 159)
Low-Fat Basic Vinaigrette (page 156)

Pasta Salads with Seafood

Pasta Salads with Seafood

Americans are eating more fish as a low-fat alternative to red meat. Shrimp is very low in fat and does not have the high amounts of cholesterol once ascribed to it. And while salmon is higher in fat that many other fish, it is still lower than red meat. Moreover the fat in salmon is a so-called "good" fat. Squid is high in cholesterol, and we do not use it in these recipes.

For tuna salads, use solid white albacore tuna packed in water. Find the freshest fish and shellfish possible for the other recipes; we have included two different methods for steaming mussels and clams.

Steamed Mussels #1

*S*crub mussels thoroughly and cut off the "beard." Discard any with opened or cracked shells. Cover with cold water and 1 tablespoon salt. Soak for 20 minutes. Preheat oven to 450 degrees. Arrange the drained mussels in one layer on a baking sheet and steam in oven for 7 to 8 minutes until the shells have opened. Discard any unopened mussels.

Steamed Mussels #2

*C*lean the mussels as in method #1. Place in a heavy kettle or pot with ½ cup dry white wine, cover and cook at high heat for 5 minutes. Leave the cover on for another 5 minutes. Discard any unopened mussels.

Steamed Clams #1

*W*ash clams thoroughly, cover with cold salted water. Discard any cracked or open shells. Let stand 15 minutes, rinse and repeat two more times. Place in a large kettle, add 2 cups boiling water, cover and bring to a boil. Reduce heat and steam for 10 minutes. Drain; discard any unopened shells.

Steamed Clams #2

*S*crub the clams thoroughly with a stiff brush under cold running water. Discard any cracked or open shells. Preheat the oven to 450 degrees. Arrange the clams in a single layer on a baking sheet and steam in oven for 7 to 8 minutes or until the shells have opened. Discard any unopened shells.

Pasta and Tuna, Simple and Nice

This colorful yet simple pasta salad would make fine luncheon fare, served, perhaps, with crunchy breadsticks and a cool fruit juice spritzer or lemonade.

10 ounces short pasta, such as shells, elbows or rigatoni
1 7-ounce can water-pack tuna, drained and chunked
1 red pepper, cut into matchsticks
½ pound broccoli, broken into bite-sized florets
3 tablespoons Parmesan cheese
¼ cup shredded fresh basil
Salt and freshly ground pepper to taste

Dressing
⅓ cup low-fat mayonnaise
2-3 tablespoons tomato sauce
¼ cup vegetable broth

Cook pasta until al dente, drain, rinse with cold water and drain again.

Blanch the broccoli in a large amount of boiling water for 2 minutes. Drain and plunge into ice water to stop the cooking and set the color, drain again. Pat dry with paper towels.

In a small bowl blend the dressing ingredients.

In a large, attractive serving bowl, toss the salad ingredients, dressing and salt and pepper to taste. Refrigerate at least 1 hour. Just before serving toss again and adjust seasonings as necessary.

Serves 6.

Tuna, Broccoli and Red Peppers with Farfalle

*I*n *Italian farfalle means butterfly. This pasta salad is as colorful as the butterflies of Southern Italy and is stunning on a buffet table at any season of the year.*

8 ounces farfalle (bow ties)
½ bunch broccoli
3 red peppers, cut into 1-inch squares, or 1 green pepper and 4 ounces of jarred roasted
    peppers, diced
2 7-ounce cans water-pack tuna, drained and broken into large chunks
12 cured green olives, pitted and halved

Dressing
¼ cup olive oil
3 tablespoons red wine vinegar
1 tablespoon water
2 tablespoons capers, drained and rinsed, chopped if large
1 teaspoon oregano, crushed, or 1 tablespoon fresh oregano
2 cloves garlic, minced
½ teaspoon salt, or to taste
¼ teaspoon freshly ground pepper

Cook pasta until al dente. Drain, rinse with cold water and drain again.

In a small bowl whisk all dressing ingredients together.

Cut broccoli stems from florets, peel the top 2 inches and slice into ½-inch pieces. Break the florets into 1-inch pieces. Blanch the stems in boiling water for 2 minutes, add the florets and blanch 1 minute. Remove with a slotted spoon and plunge into cold water and drain thoroughly. Pat dry with paper towels. Wrap the florets in plastic wrap and refrigerate.

In a large bowl gently mix the pasta, broccoli stems, peppers, olives, tuna and the dressing. Cover and chill about 2 hours before serving.

Toss the salad before serving and taste for seasoning. Make a border with the florets around the edge of the salad, then serve.

Serves 6.

Pasta Salad with Tuna and Greek Olives

_____

_____

_____

An easy and refreshing salad for lunch or dinner; accompany with a hot or cold soup and crisp flat bread.

12 ounces rigatoni, penne, or other short pasta
1 7-ounce can water-pack tuna, drained
1/4 pound large black Greek olives, pitted and chopped
1/2 box cherry tomatoes, cut in half if large
1/4 cup olive oil
1 tablespoon water
4 tablespoons fresh lemon juice
2 tablespoons capers, rinsed and drained
1/2 teaspoon oregano, crushed
1/2 teaspoon salt
1/4 teaspoon freshly ground pepper

Cook pasta until al dente, drain, rinse with cold water and drain again.

Break tuna into chunks. Put tuna, olives, olive oil, lemon juice, water, capers and salt and pepper into a small bowl and mix well.

In a large serving bowl toss pasta, tuna mixture and tomatoes. Cover and refrigerate until serving time. Taste for seasoning before serving.

Serves 6.

Tuscany Tuna, Bean and Pasta Salad

To the classic Italian bean and tuna combination we've added pasta.

8 ounces small pasta shells
1 16-ounce can small white beans, rinsed and drained
2 7-ounce cans water-pack tuna, drained and broken into small chunks
1 medium red onion, chopped
2 tablespoons chopped parsley

Dressing
1/4 cup olive oil
2 tablespoons fresh lemon juice
1/2 teaspoon sage, crushed
1 clove garlic, minced
1/2 teaspoon salt
1/4 teaspoon freshly ground pepper

Cook pasta until al dente, drain, rinse with cold water and drain again.

Mix all dressing ingredients in a large bowl. Add pasta, tuna, beans, onions and parsley and mix well.

Refrigerate at least 2 hours; stir occasionally.

Before serving taste for seasonings and toss again.

Serves 6.

Tuna, Pasta and White Bean Salad

Another tuna and bean salad, this one with a fat-free creamy dressing and raw spinach leaves.

8 ounces penne or rigatoni
1 16-ounce can small white beans, drained and rinsed
2 7-ounce cans water-pack tuna, drained and broken into chunks
4 cornichons (if available), sliced, or 2 tablespoons dill pickle, diced
1/4 cup capers, drained and rinsed
2 long mild banana peppers, seeded and cut into rings, or 1 yellow bell pepper cut into thin strips and halved
2 cups spinach leaves, washed well, drained and torn into bite-sized pieces

Dressing
1/2 cup fat-free yogurt
1/4 cup lemon juice
2 tablespoons chopped chives or green onion tops
1/2 teaspoon sugar
1/2 teaspoon basil, crushed
1/2 teaspoon salt
1/4 teaspoon freshly ground pepper

Cook pasta until al dente, drain, rinse with cold water and drain again.

Combine pasta with beans, tuna, cornichons, capers, peppers and spinach. Cover and chill.

Whisk all the dressing ingredients together in a small bowl. Cover and chill.

At serving time toss the salad with the dressing. Taste for seasonings and adjust.

Serves 6.

Rotelle and Tuna with Broccoli

*T*his *corkscrew-shaped pasta will trap the tasty bits of tuna and vegetables.*
Serve with breadsticks and vegetable sticks. A perfect picnic spread.

10 ounces rotelle
1 7-ounce can water-pack tuna, drained and flaked
2 cups broccoli florets
1 red pepper, coarsely chopped
1 cup watercress leaves and small stems
1 small red onion, thinly sliced

Dressing
1/4 cup olive or canola oil
3 tablespoons herb or white wine vinegar
1 tablespoon water
1/2 teaspoon salt
1/2 teaspoon sugar
1/2 teaspoon crushed red pepper flakes

Cook pasta until al dente, drain, rinse with cold water and drain again.

Blanch broccoli 1 minute in boiling water, remove with a slotted spoon into ice water and drain. Pat dry with paper towels.

Whisk together dressing ingredients in a small bowl.

Add tuna, broccoli, pepper, watercress, onion and dressing to pasta and toss gently but thoroughly. Taste for seasonings. Serve at room temperature or lightly chilled.

Serves 6.

Tuna and Carrot Pasta Salad

Search out unusual shapes of macaroni-type pasta and use one in this simple-to-construct salad.

8 ounces short pasta of your choice
1 7-ounce can water-pack tuna, drained and chunked
1 cup thinly sliced carrots
½ cup thinly sliced celery
4 green onions, thinly sliced
½ cup chopped dill pickles
Whites of 2 hard-cooked eggs, chopped
⅓ cup Low-Fat Creamy Garlic Dressing (page 166)
Salt and freshly ground pepper, to taste

Cook pasta until almost al dente and add sliced carrots for last two minutes of cooking. Drain, rinse with cold water and drain again. Cover and refrigerate at least 1 hour.

Add tuna, celery, pickles, onions, egg whites and the Low-Fat Creamy Garlic Dressing. Mix well, taste for salt and pepper and serve.

Serves 6.

Fettuccine with Tuna

A sophisticated salad that is a far cry from the tuna and noodle salads we ate as children.

12 ounces fettuccine
¼ cup olive or canola oil
2 cloves garlic, minced
2 tablespoons pine nuts
1 cup roughly chopped tomatoes, skinned and seeded
13-ounce can water-pack tuna, drained, broken into small chunks
½ red or green pepper, thinly sliced
6 black olives, pitted and coarsely chopped
2 tablespoons chopped parsley
3 tablespoons red wine or herb vinegar
Salt and freshly ground pepper to taste

Heat the oil in a skillet and saute the pine nuts over low heat about 3 minutes, or until nuts are golden; add garlic and saute 1 minute longer. Add tomatoes and cook briefly. Turn mixture into a large serving bowl to cool. Do not refrigerate.

Cook fettuccine until al dente, drain well. Add to the tomato mixture and toss gently. Add the tuna, pepper strips, olives, parsley and vinegar. Toss gently and season with salt and plenty of pepper. Serve at room temperature.

Serves 6.

Tuna and Garden Delight Farfalle Salad

*T*oday's supermarkets carry these garden vegetables all year round, so you won't have to wait for summer to enjoy this tasty and nutritious salad.

8 ounces farfalle (bow tie) pasta
1 13-ounce can water-pack tuna, drained and flaked
½ pound broccoli, florets only
1 pound zucchini, quartered and thinly sliced
½ pound mushrooms, thinly sliced
2 cloves garlic, minced
2 medium tomatoes, cut in thin wedges, or 12 cherry tomatoes, halved
1 medium red onion, thinly sliced
¼ cup olive or canola oil
½ teaspoon oregano, crushed
1 tablespoon chopped fresh basil or 1 teaspoon dried basil, crushed
½ cup fat-free yogurt
Salt and pepper to taste

Cook pasta until al dente, drain, rinse with cold water and drain again.

Heat oil and lightly saute broccoli, zucchini and mushrooms for 2 minutes.

Add minced garlic and herbs, sprinkle with salt and pepper and saute 1 minute longer.

Add vegetables to pasta with tuna, tomatoes and onions. Mix lightly and add yogurt to moisten. Taste for salt and pepper. Serve at room temperature or lightly chilled.

Serves 6.

Tart Tuna and Orzo Salad

*A*fter finishing all those Saturday morning chores, reward yourself with this easy and tasty salad for lunch.

1½ cups orzo, ditali or other tiny pasta
1 7-ounce can water-pack tuna, drained and flaked
1 small red onion, thinly sliced
1 medium to large tomato, seeded and coarsely chopped
½ cup chopped parsley
1 teaspoon oregano or basil, crushed
3 cups iceberg lettuce in ½-inch wide slices

Dressing
⅓ cup olive or canola oil
2 tablespoons lemon juice
2 tablespoons herb or white wine vinegar
1 tablespoon water
½ teaspoon salt
½ teaspoon freshly ground pepper or to taste

Cook pasta until al dente, drain, rinse with cold water and drain again.

Mix dressing ingredients in a small bowl.

Add remaining ingredients, except lettuce, to pasta. Pour on half the dressing and toss well. Taste for seasonings and add a tablespoon or more of dressing as needed.

Make a bed of the sliced lettuce on a deep platter, drizzle with remaining dressing and mound the pasta salad in the center.

Serves 6.

Salmon and Pasta with Carrots and Watercress

*B*right colors but subtle flavors and textures.

8 ounces wheel pasta or small shells
½ pound salmon steak, simmered 8 minutes in:
    ½ cup dry white wine
    ½ cup water
    6 sprigs parsley
    1 bay leaf
    1 clove garlic
    1 teaspoon salt
3 or 4 carrots, thinly sliced
½ bunch watercress, coarse stems removed
12 cured black or green olives, pitted and halved
2 tablespoons capers, rinsed and chopped if large

Dressing
¼ cup olive or canola oil
¼ cup lemon juice
1 tablespoon water
2 teaspoons Dijon mustard
1 clove garlic, minced
1 teaspoon tarragon, crushed
½ teaspoon sugar
½ teaspoon salt
¼ teaspoon freshly ground pepper

Cook pasta until al dente, drain, rinse with cold water and drain again.

Cook salmon as directed. Remove skin and bones, coarsely flake and refrigerate.

Blanch carrots in boiling water for 2 minutes, remove with a slotted spoon, plunge into ice water and drain. Pat dry with paper towels.

In a large attractive bowl mix the dressing ingredients and add the pasta, chilled salmon, carrots, watercress, olives and capers. Toss gently and chill lightly before serving.

Serves 6.

Summer Salmon and Shells

A salad to remind you of summer. A nice luncheon dish served with a hot but crisp green vegetable, French bread and iced tea.

8 ounces small shell pasta
2 cups shredded iceberg lettuce
12 cured ripe olives, pitted and halved
½ box cherry tomatoes, halved
2 medium cucumbers, peeled, halved and seeded, then sliced thinly into half-rounds
1 large can red salmon, drained, skin and bones removed, and chunked

Dressing
⅓ cup low-fat mayonnaise
3 tablespoons skim milk
2 tablespoon vinegar
1½ tablespoon finely chopped onion
½ teaspoon dillweed
½ teaspoon salt, or to taste
¼ teaspoon freshly ground pepper, or to taste

Mix dressing ingredients together and chill. Cook pasta until al dente, drain, rinse with cold water and drain again. Cover and chill.

In a large glass bowl, layer lettuce and pasta and spread with half the dressing. Layer olives, tomatoes, cucumbers and salmon and spread remaining dressing over the top, cover with plastic wrap and chill about 1 hour.

Toss at the table and serve.

Serves 6.

Any Season Salmon and Shell Salad

*Y*ou *probably have the makings for this salad in your cupboard or refrigerator right now. If not, substitutions are allowed.*

8 ounces shell pasta (or other macaroni type)
1 large can red salmon, drained, skin and bones removed, and flaked
1 cup thinly sliced carrots
½ cup chopped celery
½ cup pimento-stuffed olives, halved
½ package frozen peas, blanched with boiling water and well drained
1 small onion, chopped, or 4 green onions thinly sliced
½ red or green pepper, julienned

Dressing
¼ cup olive or canola oil
3 tablespoons lemon juice
1 tablespoon white wine or herb vinegar
1 tablespoon water
2 teaspoons Dijon mustard
1 tablespoon fresh dillweed, chopped, or 1 teaspoon dried dillweed
½ teaspoon sugar
½ teaspoon salt
¼ teaspoon freshly ground pepper

Cook pasta until almost al dente, add carrot slices and cook 2 minutes. Drain, rinse with cold water and drain again. Cover and chill.

Whisk dressing ingredients in a small bowl. Add salmon, celery, olives, peas, parsley, onions, peppers and almost all the dressing to the pasta and carrots.

Cover and chill another ½ hour before serving.

Before serving toss salad, taste for seasoning and add remaining dressing.

Serves 6.

Fish and Thin Noodles, Asian Style

An economical but impressive dish to wow your dinner guests. Chinese noodles, sesame oil and fresh bean sprouts can be found in large supermarkets and Asian food stores.

8 ounces spaghettini or thin Chinese egg noodles
1½ pounds firm fish fillets: cod, haddock, orange roughy
¼ cup lemon juice
1 tablespoon canola or vegetable oil
2 teaspoons sesame oil
2 cups fresh bean sprouts
1 large carrot, coarsely shredded
¼ cup chopped green onion tops

Dressing
⅓ cup chicken broth
¼ cup soy sauce
2 tablespoons low-fat peanut butter
2 teaspoons sesame oil
1 tablespoon white wine or rice vinegar
1 teaspoon sugar
2 teaspoons minced garlic
2 teaspoons minced fresh ginger root
¼ teaspoon Tabasco sauce, or to taste

Put the fillets, lemon juice and water to cover in a skillet and poach, at barely a simmer, for 5 to 7 minutes. Remove with a slotted spoon, cover with plastic wrap and cool. Remove skin if necessary and flake. Cover and set aside.

Cook the pasta until al dente, drain and transfer to a large serving bowl. Toss with 1 tablespoon oil and 2 teaspoons sesame oil.

Blanch bean sprouts in boiling water for 30 seconds. Drain and rinse with cold water and drain again. Pat dry with paper towels.

In a small bowl mix the dressing ingredients together.

Arrange the bean sprouts and shredded carrots over the noodles. Top with the flaked fish. Pour the dressing on top and garnish with the chopped green onion tops. Serve lightly chilled; do not toss before serving.

Serves 6.

Seaside Spaghetti

On a warm summer day this melange of flavors will remind you of the sunny Mediterranean. Serve with crisp Italian bread to sop up the flavorful juices.

12 ounces spaghetti or linguine
1/2 pound fillet of sole or flounder
1/2 pound small raw shrimp
6 garden-fresh tomatoes, peeled, seeded and coarsely chopped or 1 16-ounce can plum
    tomatoes, drained and coarsely chopped
1/4 cup olive or canola oil
1 medium onion, finely chopped
3 cloves garlic, minced
1/4 cup dry white wine
1 tablespoon fresh basil, chopped or 1 1/2 teaspoons dried basil, crushed
2 teaspoons fresh marjoram or 1 teaspoon dried marjoram, crushed
Salt and pepper to taste
1/2 cup chopped parsley

Cook pasta until al dente, drain, rinse with cold water and drain again.

Poach fish fillet in lightly salted water with a bay leaf, about 3 minutes. Cool and flake, then cover and set aside.

Cook shrimp in boiling salted water with a small onion for 2 minutes, drain, shell, then cover while cooling.

Saute onion in oil until barely tender, add garlic and cook briefly. Add wine and herbs and cook about 1 minute. Add tomatoes and cook 5 minutes over medium heat. Add salt and pepper to taste. (Remember that cold sauce needs heavier seasoning.) Refrigerate until cold, then gently fold in fish and shrimp.

Arrange pasta on a deep platter, spoon seafood sauce on top and sprinkle with chopped fresh parsley.

Serves 6.

Seafood, Pasta and Vegetable Salad

If shrimp is too costly, substitute less-expensive large scallops, sliced after cooking. To make up for the color the shrimp would have provided, add a small jar of drained, sliced pimento.

8 ounces rotelle
1 pound flounder fillets
1/2 pound small shrimp
1/2 cup dry white wine
1/4 cup chopped green onions
1/2 teaspoon salt
2 medium zucchini, cut into 2-inch lengths and julienned
2 leeks, white part only, sliced thinly
1 1/2 cups frozen peas, thawed

Dressing
1 cup peeled, shredded cucumber
1/2 teaspoon salt
1/2 cup low-fat sour cream or fat-free yogurt
2 teaspoons dillweed
1/4 teaspoon freshly ground pepper
Dash of cardamom (optional)

Cook pasta until al dente, drain, rinse with cold water and drain again. Cover and chill.

Simmer the flounder in wine, scallions and salt for 3 minutes, add shrimp and simmer 2 minutes more. Remove with a slotted spoon and, when cool, flake fish and shell and devein shrimp, cover and chill.

To make dressing, mix cucumber and salt and let stand in a colander for 1 hour. Press moisture out, then mix with sour cream or yogurt, dillweed, pepper and optional cardamom.

Toss pasta, seafood, zucchini, leeks and peas with the dressing. Adjust seasonings to taste.

Serves 6.

Delicate Oriental Noodle and Seafood Salad

A light but vibrant salad perfect for a first course or a hot weather main course. Double the amount of shrimp and scallops to serve six as a main course.

8 ounces cellophane noodles or vermicelli
$\frac{1}{2}$ pound small raw shrimp
$\frac{1}{2}$ pound scallops
1 cup thinly sliced celery
1 whole pimento, sliced
1 handful watercress leaves and tender stems
1 large cucumber, halved, seeded and thinly sliced

Dressing
$\frac{1}{3}$ cup fresh lemon juice
$\frac{1}{2}$ cup chopped green onion, tops and bottoms
2 tablespoons sesame oil
1 tablespoon soy sauce
$\frac{1}{2}$ teaspoon salt
$\frac{1}{2}$ teaspoon hot chili oil or $\frac{1}{4}$ teaspoon Tabasco sauce
$\frac{1}{2}$ teaspoon sugar

In a small bowl whisk all dressing ingredients together.

Cook cellophane noodles according to package directions. Drain, rinse with cold water and drain again. Transfer to a serving bowl and toss with half the dressing.

Simmer shrimp and scallops in boiling water just to cover, about 2 minutes. Drain and cool. Shell and devein shrimp and slice scallops into $\frac{1}{2}$-inch rounds. If using bay scallops, leave them whole or cut in half.

Add shrimp and scallops, celery, pimento, watercress and the remaining dressing to the noodles. Toss gently and chill until serving time. Divide among six (preferably glass) salad plates and garnish with the cucumber slices.

Serves 6.

Rice Noodles and Shrimp with Vegetables

Start with an assortment of appetizers from your local Chinese restaurant. This Asian-style pasta salad followed by a variety of sherbets and fortune cookies makes for an easy Sunday night supper.

8 ounces rice noodles or bean thread noodles
12 ounces shrimp, cooked and peeled
10-ounce package fresh spinach, washed and torn into small pieces
$\frac{1}{4}$ pound fresh mushrooms sliced
4 green onions, sliced diagonally into $\frac{1}{2}$-inch pieces
1 medium zucchini, julienned into 1-inch lengths
8-10 radishes, sliced

Dressing
$\frac{1}{4}$ cup canola oil
1 clove garlic, minced
2 tablespoons soy sauce
2 tablespoons rice vinegar or white wine vinegar
$\frac{1}{2}$ teaspoon Chinese five-spice powder
2 teaspoons sesame seeds, for garnish

In a small bowl whisk dressing ingredients together.

Cook noodles according to package directions, drain, rinse with cold water and drain again. Toss with 1 tablespoon dressing.

Cut shrimp into 1-inch pieces. Add shrimp, spinach, mushrooms, onions, zucchini and radishes to the noodles. Toss with the dressing, cover and chill.

Sprinkle the sesame seeds on top of the salad and serve.

Serves 6.

Herb-Dressed Shrimp and Pasta Salad

*I*nfluenced by Northern Italian cuisine, this salad is enhanced by a delicate but distinctive herb dressing. It is light enough for a first course, but would do nicely as the entree on a warm summer evening.

12 ounces small twist pasta or small shells
1 pound cooked shrimp, shelled and deveined
$\frac{1}{2}$ cup chopped parsley

Dressing
$\frac{1}{4}$ cup olive or canola oil
4 tablespoons fresh lemon juice
1 tablespoon water
1 teaspoon tarragon, crushed, or if available 1 tablespoon chopped fresh tarragon
$\frac{1}{2}$ teaspoon rosemary, crushed, or $1\frac{1}{2}$ teaspoons chopped fresh rosemary
$\frac{1}{2}$ teaspoon salt, or more to taste
$\frac{1}{4}$ teaspoon freshly ground pepper, or more to taste

Cook pasta until al dente, drain, rinse with cold water and drain again. Cover and set aside to cool.

Chop the shrimp into small pieces.

In a small bowl whisk together all the dressing ingredients. Taste and adjust seasonings if needed.

In a serving bowl, toss the pasta, shrimp, parsley and dressing. Cover and let the flavors blend about $\frac{1}{2}$ hour. Refrigerate if the salad won't be served for more than $\frac{1}{2}$ hour. Just before serving toss again.

Serves 6.

Shrimp, Ham and Penne
with Dilled Vinaigrette

We are so pleased that shrimp is no longer a health no-no. The flavor, texture and pink edges are a pleasing contrast in this refreshing salad.

8 ounces penne or rotini
3/4 pound cooked, diced shrimp
1/4 pound lean ham steak, cooked and julienned
1 small red onion, thinly sliced
1 cucumber, peeled, seeded and thinly sliced
12 ripe olives, pitted and sliced
2-ounce jar sliced or diced pimento, drained
1 recipe Low-Fat Dill Vinaigrette (see page 158)

Cook pasta until al dente, drain, rinse with cold water and drain again. Cover and chill.

Add shrimp, ham, onion, cucumber, olives, pimento and the Low-Fat Dill Vinaigrette to the pasta. Toss well and serve lightly chilled.

Serves 6.

Linguine with Shrimp-Yogurt Sauce

A light and tasty first course or luncheon dish. Instead of a calorie-laden cream sauce, this recipe substitutes fat-free yogurt.

12 ounces linguine
½ pound small shrimp, cooked and peeled
½ cup chopped parsley
½ cup sliced green onions
½ cup fat-free yogurt
1 tablespoon fresh lemon juice
Salt and freshly ground pepper to taste
1 teaspoon finely grated lemon zest
1 teaspoon tarragon
½ teaspoon thyme
¼ teaspoon paprika

Cook the pasta until al dente, drain, rinse with cold water and drain again.

In a blender or food processor combine half the cooked shrimp, the yogurt, lemon juice, salt and pepper, lemon zest, tarragon, thyme and paprika. Blend until almost smooth. Taste and adjust seasonings as needed.

Toss pasta, reserved shrimp and dressing thoroughly. Let stand at room temperature about ½ hour to allow flavors to blend before serving.

Serves 6.

Orzo and Shrimp Salad

Serve this light salad in lettuce cups as a first course or to your card group or committee members for lunch or as an evening snack.

1½ cups orzo or other tiny pasta
¾ pound small or medium shrimp
2 cups simmering water seasoned with 1 teaspoon salt, 4 peppercorns, 1 stalk celery with
    leaves, 2 whole cloves
4 stalks celery with leaves, finely chopped
¼ cup minced parsley
1 tablespoon capers, rinsed, for garnish

Dressing
¼ cup fat-free yogurt
2 tablespoons olive or canola oil
3 tablespoons white wine vinegar
½ teaspoon salt
¼ teaspoon freshly ground pepper
½ teaspoon dillweed

Cook pasta until al dente, drain, rinse with cold water and drain again.

Simmer the unpeeled shrimp in the seasoned water 2-3 minutes.

Drain, cool and shell. Cut into coarse pieces. Chill.

Mix dressing ingredients and toss in serving bowl with pasta, shrimp, celery and parsley. Taste for seasoning and garnish with capers before serving. Serve lightly chilled.

Serves 6.

Pasta-and-Shrimp Stuffed Tomato Shells

A *bright red tomato shell nestled in a tender bibb lettuce leaf makes an attractive first course; with the addition of pureed carrot soup and crisp French bread, it is a satisfying luncheon entree.*

1 cup orzo or other tiny pasta
6 medium to large ripe tomatoes
¾ pound shrimp, cooked, shelled and coarsely chopped
1 large cucumber, peeled, seeded and coarsely chopped
¼ cup finely chopped red pepper
¼ cup finely chopped green onions
½ teaspoon salt
½ cup Low-Fat Dill Vinaigrette (page 158)

Hollow out tomatoes and drain well upside down. (Reserve tomato pulp for another use.) Cover and chill.

Cook pasta until al dente, drain, rinse with cold water and drain again. Mix with 1 tablespoon of the Low-Fat Dill Vinaigrette dressing.

Add the shrimp, vegetables, remaining dressing and salt to the pasta and refrigerate until well chilled.

Fill tomato shells and arrange on lettuce-lined salad plates.

Serves 6.

Jumbo Shells
Stuffed with Crabmeat

This is quite an elegant first course. Serve with lemon wedges and thinly sliced toasted French bread.

12 jumbo pasta shells (cook a few extra as a couple usually break)
1 pound crabmeat (preferably lump or backfin)
$\frac{1}{3}$ cup olive oil, divided
3 tablespoons fresh lemon juice, divided
1 tablespoon capers, rinsed and drained, chopped if large
2 tablespoons minced celery
2 tablespoons minced parsley, divided
$\frac{1}{2}$ teaspoon salt, or more to taste
$\frac{1}{8}$ teaspoon cayenne pepper
$\frac{1}{3}$ cup Low-Fat Basic Vinaigrette (page 156)
Boston or bibb lettuce leaves
Watercress sprigs, for garnish
Lemon wedges, for garnish

Cook pasta shells, gently, until al dente. Remove with a slotted spoon and drain. While still hot, mix carefully with 1 tablespoon olive oil, 1 tablespoon lemon juice and 1 tablespoon parsley.

Drain any juice from crabmeat and discard. Mix the crab with remaining olive oil, lemon juice, capers, celery, parsley, salt and cayenne. Taste for seasoning and adjust to taste. Stuff shells, cover and refrigerate until shortly before serving.

Arrange lettuce on salad plates, add two shells per plate and drizzle lightly with vinaigrette dressing. Garnish with watercress sprigs and lemon wedges.

Serves 6.

Herbed Scallops and Linguine

An elegant first course, garnished with sprigs of fresh dill and accompanied by long, thin breadsticks for texture contrast.

8 ounces linguine
1½ pounds bay scallops (about 1½ pints) or sea scallops, quartered after cooking

Dressing
½ cup low-fat mayonnaise
2 tablespoons rice vinegar
1 tablespoon capers, rinsed and drained and chopped if large
1½ tablespoons fresh herbs (dill, thyme or tarragon), chopped
2 tablespoons minced parsley
½ teaspoon salt
¼ teaspoon freshly ground pepper
Minced chives or finely chopped green onion tops for garnish
Herb sprigs for garnish

Cook pasta until al dente, drain, rinse with cold water and drain again. Wash and drain scallops. Place them in a large skillet and barely cover with cold water. Bring to a boil, lower heat and simmer 1 minute. Drain and refrigerate while preparing the dressing.

Whisk the dressing ingredients together and combine with the scallops. Refrigerate if not using immediately.

At serving time mix the scallops gently with the linguine and divide among six salad plates. Sprinkle with chives and garnish with dill or other herb sprigs. Serve chilled.

Serves 6.

Fettuccine with Scallops and Langostinos

Scallops marinated in lime juice, langostinos and a piquant dressing of lime and fresh coriander make this salad a refreshing first course for summer parties.

12 ounces fettuccine
½ pound bay scallops
1 12-ounce package frozen langostinos or jumbo shrimp
1 cup fresh lime juice, divided
¼ cup olive or canola oil
Salt and freshly ground pepper to taste
Pinch of sugar
2 tablespoons chopped fresh coriander

Marinate scallops in ⅔ cup lime juice 3 to 4 hours or overnight in the refrigerator.

Defrost langostinos, rinse with cold water and pat dry. Or shell and cook shrimp in seasoned water 3 minutes, drain and pat dry.

Cook pasta until al dente, drain, rinse with cold water and drain again.

Drain scallops and discard marinade.

Mix ⅓ cup lime juice, oil, salt, pepper and sugar in a small bowl. Add finely chopped coriander. Taste for seasoning.

Add all ingredients to pasta and toss lightly. Serve at room temperature or lightly chilled.

Serves 6.

Scallop, Green Bean and Wagonwheel Salad

*F*resh dill is a must for optimum enjoyment of this refreshing seafood salad.

8 ounces wheels or shells
1½ pounds large sea scallops
1 cup dry white wine
1 small onion, sliced
2 lemon slices
1 bay leaf
½ pound green beans, cooked 2 minutes and chilled
4 scallions, sliced into rounds, including some of the green
Red or green lettuce leaves
Radicchio leaves, for garnish, if available

Dressing
⅓ cup olive or canola oil
¼ cup white wine vinegar
1 tablespoon water
1 teaspoon salt
Freshly ground pepper to taste
1 teaspoon sugar
2 tablespoons chopped fresh dillweed
½ teaspoon dill seed

Mix together all dressing ingredients first; the dressing should stand at room temperature several hours to let the flavor develop. Whisk before using on salad and adjust seasonings to taste.

Cook wagonwheels until al dente, drain, rinse with cold water and drain again.

Simmer scallops in the wine, onion, lemon, bay leaf and water to barely cover, for 5 minutes. Cool in liquid, then drain. Slice scallops thinly. Toss with the pasta, beans and scallions. Pour the dressing over the salad and toss. Serve lightly chilled or at room temperature on the lettuce leaves.

Serves 6.

Curried Mussel Salad with Tiny Pasta

Use the smallest size pasta you can find, such as ave maria, ditalini, rigati or orzo. However, in a pinch, the smallest shells will do.

1½ cups tiny pasta
4 quarts steamed mussels (page 64)
½ 10-ounce package frozen tiny peas, thawed
½ cup chopped celery leaves or parsley, for garnish

Curried French Dressing
⅓ cup olive or canola oil
2 tablespoons wine vinegar
1 tablespoon minced green onion
1 teaspoon curry powder, or more to taste
½ teaspoon salt, or more to taste

Cook the pasta until al dente, drain, rinse with cold water and drain again.

Pour boiling water over the peas and drain.

In a large shallow bowl combine the pasta with the peas and mussels and toss with the dressing. Cover and chill at least 2 hours.

Taste for seasoning before serving, then sprinkle with the chopped celery or parsley.

Serves 6.

Mussels Marinara with Linguine

A *tantalizing blend of rich Italian seasonings combined with inexpensive mussels and pasta. Italian bread to dip in the flavorful sauce and a crisp green salad will make a satisfying meal for family or friends.*

12 ounces linguine
4 quarts mussels
1 large onion, thinly sliced
3 cloves garlic, minced
¼ cup olive oil
1 lemon, thinly sliced
1 28-ounce can Italian plum tomatoes, including juice
3 tablespoons chopped fresh basil, or 2 teaspoons dried basil, crushed
1 teaspoon oregano, crushed
⅛ teaspoon cayenne pepper
½ teaspoon freshly ground pepper
1½ teaspoons salt
½ cup dry red wine
Chopped Italian flat-leaf parsley for garnish, or regular parsley if Italian is not available

Clean the mussels, following the directions given on page 64.

Saute the onion and garlic in the olive oil in a large pot. Add the lemon slices when the onion is soft. Coarsely chop the tomatoes in a food processor or mash with a fork to break up. Add to the pot with the basil, oregano, cayenne, black pepper and salt. Simmer over low heat, stirring occasionally, about 25 minutes. Add the wine and simmer 15 to 20 minutes more.

Cook the linguine until al dente and drain well. Turn into a shallow bowl and toss with 2 tablespoons of the simmering sauce.

While the pasta is cooking, add the cleaned mussels to the simmering sauce and cook about 6 to 8 minutes, until the shells open. Discard any unopened shells. Pour the sauce over the pasta and mix gently. Allow to stand at room temperature about 1 hour before serving. Sprinkle with the chopped parsley and serve.

Serves 6.

Mussels and Pasta in Sauce Verte

A first course of distinction, this dish uses two of the basic sauces found in the chapter on dressings.

8 ounces medium shells
18-24 fresh, tightly closed mussels
½ cup water
1 cloves garlic, crushed
¼ cup Low-Fat Basic Vinaigrette (page 156)
½ cup Low-Fat Sauce Verte (page 164)

Cook pasta until al dente, drain well and toss with the Low-Fat Basic Vinaigrette. Cover and refrigerate at least 1 hour.

Clean the mussels following the directions on page 64. Place the mussels in a large skillet, add water and garlic. Cook, covered, over high heat 5 to 8 minutes. Shake skillet frequently so mussels will cook uniformly. When mussels open, remove with a slotted spoon to a large bowl. Discard any unopened mussels. Cover and refrigerate 1 hour.

Prepare Low-Fat Sauce Verte. Put 1 teaspoon sauce on each chilled mussel in shell. Reserve remaining sauce.

Turn chilled pasta onto a serving platter and mound filled mussels in the middle. Pass reserved sauce.

Six appetizer servings.

Shell Pasta with
Mussels and Broccoli

*H*ere *is an inexpensive but sophisticated salad that will be a crowd-pleaser on summer buffet tables.*

8 ounces shell pasta
4 quarts mussels
½ pound broccoli
¼ pound mushrooms, thinly sliced
2 cloves garlic, minced
4 green onions, chopped
1 teaspoon tarragon, crushed
1 teaspoon thyme, crushed
1 cup dry white wine
2 teaspoons salt
2 tablespoons chopped parsley, for garnish

Dressing
½ cup liquid from mussels
3 tablespoons olive or canola oil
1½ teaspoons Dijon mustard
½ teaspoon freshly ground pepper
Salt to taste

Clean the mussels following the directions on page 64. Transfer the mussels to a stainless steel pot and add the garlic, onions, herbs, salt and wine. Bring to a boil, cover, reduce heat and steam 5 to 8 minutes or until the shells have opened. Remove the mussels and discard any unopened shells. Strain the liquid, return to the pot and reduce to ½ cup. Reserve for the dressing.

Cook the pasta until al dente, drain, rinse with cold water and drain again.

Cut away the heavy bottom stems on the broccoli and peel the remaining stems. Slice the stems into ¼-inch matchsticks and break the heads into small florets. Cook in boiling, salted water for 1 minute. Drain, rinse with cold water, drain again and pat dry with paper towels.

Remove the cooled mussels from the shells and add to the pasta with the broccoli, mushrooms and the dressing. Mix well and refrigerate. Before serving taste for seasoning, then sprinkle with chopped parsley and toss gently.

Serves 6.

Shells with Shrimp, Scallops and Snow Peas

This light and tangy salad will whet any appetite when served as a first course. Or it can stand alone as a refreshing luncheon dish.

8 ounces shell pasta
1 pound small or medium shrimp
1 small onion
4 peppercorns
2 teaspoons salt
1 pound scallops
¼ pound snow peas or ½ 10-ounce box frozen snow peas
2 cucumbers, peeled, seeded and thinly sliced
4 celery stalks, thinly sliced

Dressing
½ cup rice vinegar
3 tablespoons olive or canola oil
¼ cup light soy sauce
3 tablespoons dry sherry
1 tablespoon sesame oil
1 tablespoon water
2 teaspoons dry mustard
1 teaspoon sugar
2 teaspoons toasted sesame seeds

Cook shrimp in boiling water with onion, peppercorns and salt about 3 minutes. Drain, cool and peel. Cook scallops in lightly salted, simmering water just until translucent and drain. If using large sea scallops, quarter; then add scallops to shrimp and set aside to cool.

Put fresh or thawed snow peas in a colander and pour boiling water over them, drain and pat dry with paper towels. Transfer to a bowl and toss with the sliced cucumbers and celery.

Cook pasta until al dente, drain, rinse with cold water and drain again.

While the pasta is cooking, combine dressing ingredients. Add the shrimp and scallops to the vegetables and toss with half the dressing.

Arrange the drained pasta in a shallow bowl and toss with the remaining dressing. Mound the seafood and vegetable mixture in the center of the pasta. Serve at room temperature or lightly chilled.

Serves 6.

Linguine and
Mixed Seafood Salad

A special trip to the fishmonger — preferably the wharf — is well worth it for this stunning summertime treat.

8 ounces linguine
1 pound small shrimp
3 quarts mussels
2 pounds littleneck clams or other small hard-shelled clams
1 small red onion, thinly sliced
⅓ cup chopped Italian flat-leaf or regular parsley

Dressing
¼ cup fresh lemon juice
4 tablespoons olive or canola oil
2 cloves garlic, minced
½ teaspoon salt
¼ teaspoon freshly ground pepper

Cook the linguine until al dente, drain, rinse with cold water and drain again.

In a small bowl whisk together the dressing ingredients and set aside.

Clean and cook the mussels and clams following the directions on pages 64–65. Do not shell.

Wash and peel the shrimp. Spray a large non-stick skillet with olive oil cooking spray and saute the shrimp over medium heat about 2 minutes. Transfer to a large serving bowl, preferably glass.

To the bowl add the pasta, the steamed mussels and steamed clams. Toss with the salad dressing and chill at least 3 hours. Before serving taste for salt and pepper and adjust to taste.

Add onion rings and parsley and toss again.

Serves 6.

Fusilli and Mussels in Spinach Sauce

*H*ere is an elegant — or earthy — accompaniment to your next seafood
dinner or buffet table. All the preparations are done early in the day and it's
just toss-and-serve at the last minute.

12 ounces fusilli or linguine
4 quarts mussels
1 cup dry white wine
¼ cup lemon juice
½ cup chopped parsley
1 teaspoon grated fresh ginger root
1 teaspoon salt

Spinach Sauce
1½ cups tightly packed fresh spinach, coarse stems removed
½ cup parsley, coarse stems removed
6 green onions, cut into 1-inch pieces
½ cup fat-free yogurt
2 tablespoons low-fat mayonnaise
¼ cup fresh lemon juice
½ teaspoon grated fresh ginger root
1 teaspoon salt
½ teaspoon freshly ground pepper

Clean and cook the mussels with the wine, lemon juice, parsley, ginger
and salt following the directions on page 64. Remove with a slotted
spoon, strain and reserve broth. Cool mussels and remove from their
shells. Cover and refrigerate with some of the cooking broth. Discard
remaining broth.

Cook pasta until al dente, drain, rinse with cold water and drain again.
Cover and refrigerate.

In a food processor or blender puree the spinach, parsley and green
onions. Add the remaining ingredients and blend thoroughly. Cover and
refrigerate.

At serving time toss the pasta with about ¼ cup of the sauce. Drain
mussels and mix with ½ cup of the sauce. Top the pasta with the mussels
and pass the remaining Spinach Sauce.

Serves 6.

Pasta Salads with Poultry

Pasta Salads with Poultry

Skinless and boneless chicken breasts are a boon to low-fat and low-calorie eating. The secret to achieving the succulence called for in these recipes is very gentle poaching of the chicken pieces.

For ease of preparation, these recipes use boneless, skinless chicken breasts unless otherwise indicated. However, we personally prefer cooking bone-in chicken breasts for the added flavor they provide. The flavorful broth can be stored in the freezer, then used in homemade soups or added to chicken casserole recipes.

After removing any skin and visible fat, cook chicken breasts (boneless or bone-in) in seasoned water for about 15 minutes. Keep the water just below the simmer (a slight surface shimmering is ideal); that way the meat turns out juicy and succulent. High heat tends to produce stringy and dry chicken. Remove the chicken from the liquid, let cool, and proceed with your favorite recipe.

Indonesian Spaghetti and Chicken Salad

An exotic-sounding recipe that's both simple to make and delicious. The dressing ingredients can be found at Asian food stores and in the gourmet section of most supermarkets.

8 ounces dried oriental whole-wheat noodles or the same amount of thin spaghetti
1 whole boneless, skinless chicken breast
1 pound fresh peas, shelled or 1 10-ounce package frozen peas, thawed
¼ pound radishes, sliced
2 cucumbers, peeled

Dressing
¼ cup low-fat peanut butter
6 tablespoons soy sauce
3 tablespoons white wine vinegar
10 drops hot chili oil
12 drops sesame oil
⅛ cup water

Cook oriental noodles for 4 minutes in boiling water or if, using spaghetti, until al dente; drain, rinse with cold water and drain again. Do not refrigerate.

Poach the chicken breast in a small amount of water for about 15 minutes. Cool and cut into strips, 1½ × ½ inches. Cut cucumbers in half lengthwise and remove seeds. Slice into thin half-rounds.

Parboil fresh peas or pour boiling water over thawed frozen peas; drain thoroughly.

In a large bowl combine noodles, chicken, peas, sliced radishes and cucumber slices.

In a small bowl combine the dressing ingredients and add to the salad. Mix well and serve at room temperature.

Serves 6.

Cold Chicken and Noodles in a Spicy Sauce

This sesame sauce is particularly tasty. A delicious meal might include this salad, green beans vinaigrette and seasoned French bread rounds crisped in the oven. End the meal with the surprising and satisfying combination of lemon sherbet and hot fudge sauce (low-fat, of course).

12 ounces linguine
3 boneless, skinless chicken breast halves
1 tablespoon sesame oil

Sauce
½ cup low-fat peanut butter
4 tablespoons water
1 teaspoon Chinese hot oil
5 tablespoons soy sauce
3 tablespoons white wine vinegar
¼ cup chicken broth (or poaching liquid)
2 tablespoons minced garlic

Poach chicken breasts in seasoned simmering water until just tender, about 15 minutes. Cool and tear or cut meat into thin strips.

Cook linguine to al dente stage, drain well and toss with the sesame oil.

Blend the peanut butter with the water. Add the rest of the sauce ingredients and mix well.

Combine warm linguine, chicken and sauce. Chill at least four hours. Remove from the refrigerator about ½ hour before serving.

Serves 6.

Chinese Noodle and Chicken Salad with Peanut Sauce

A visual treat and almost a complete meal on a platter. Add a jellied consomme or hot clear broth for the first course and sliced kiwi and strawberries to round out your menu.

8 ounces thin Chinese egg noodles or spaghetti
1 pound boneless, skinless chicken breasts
1 small onion
1 stalk celery
1 bay leaf
½ teaspoon salt
2 cups chicken broth
2 teaspoons sesame oil

Vegetable Garnish
1 cup fresh bean sprouts, blanched and drained
1 cup thinly sliced carrot
1 cup thinly sliced, seeded cucumber
½ cup sliced green onions
1 15-ounce can baby corn on the cob, drained and rinsed

Creamy Peanut Sauce
⅓ cup smooth low-fat peanut butter
⅔ cup chicken broth
¼ cup soy sauce
2 tablespoons sesame oil
2 tablespoons minced garlic
2 tablespoons minced fresh ginger
2 tablespoons sugar
2 tablespoons red wine vinegar
1 teaspoon hot chili oil, or more to taste

Cook the noodles until al dente, drain, rinse with cold water and drain again. Simmer the chicken breast with 2 cups broth, salt, onion, celery and bay leaf for 15 minutes and cool in the stock; then shred. Reduce the stock, after straining, to about ⅔ cup. Reserve for the sauce.

On a large platter toss the noodles with the chicken and sesame oil. Garnish with vegetables. Mix the dressing ingredients In a food processor fitted with the steel blade or in a blender.

Transfer the sauce to a sauce boat and pass with the oriental platter. Serve the salad at room temperature or lightly chilled.

Serves 6.

Chinese Noodle and Mushroom Salad with Chicken

The Chinese mushrooms in this salad are worth tracking down; the larger supermarkets sometimes have them and Asian markets always do.

12 ounces fine Chinese egg noodles or vermicelli
6 large black Chinese mushrooms (soaked in warm water for 20 minutes)
8 ounces boneless, skinless chicken breast, poached until tender and shredded
½ cup smoked ham, trimmed of fat, julienned (optional)
½ can water chestnuts, rinsed and sliced
¼ cup sliced green onions
3 tablespoons chopped cilantro (parsley can be substituted)

Dressing
2 tablespoons olive oil
2 tablespoons sesame oil
1 teaspoon hot chili oil (or to taste)
4 tablespoons soy sauce
3 tablespoons cider vinegar

Cook the noodles or vermicelli until al dente, drain, rinse with cold water and drain again.

Drain mushrooms, squeeze and pat dry. Discard stems and slice caps.

Combine the dressing ingredients in a small bowl. Add the mushrooms and remaining ingredients to the noodles, pour the dressing over and toss to coat thoroughly. Taste for seasoning.

Serve at room temperature or lightly chilled.

Serves 6.

Stir-Fried Chicken, Linguine and Peanuts

Another one-dish meal with Asian overtones. To make scallion brushes, cut tops off 6 scallions, leaving about 2-3 inches of green. Cut root ends off, then slice white part of scallions in fine strips almost to green part. Place scallions in cold water until ends open and curl slightly.

12 ounces linguine
1 pound boneless, skinless chicken breasts, thinly sliced
1 tablespoon cornstarch
3 tablespoons olive or canola oil, divided
4 scallions, sliced on the diagonal into 1-inch pieces
1 clove garlic, finely minced
4 carrots, peeled and sliced on the diagonal into $\frac{1}{2}$-inch pieces and quickly blanched until crisp-tender
2 green peppers, cut into thin strips
1 cup chicken broth, or one chicken bouillon cube in one cup of water
3 tablespoons dry sherry or dry vermouth
3 tablespoons soy sauce
2 tablespoons firmly packed dark brown sugar
$\frac{1}{4}$ cup peanuts, chopped
6 scallion brushes, if desired (see above)

Cook linguine until al dente, drain, and rinse with cold water and drain again.

In wok or large frying pan, stir-fry green pepper, scallions and garlic in oil for about one minute. Push to one side. Combine chicken with cornstarch. Add chicken to wok and stir-fry until browned. Add carrots and mix vegetables and meat together; cook about 1 more minute.

Mix soy sauce, sherry and brown sugar with chicken broth. Add to mixture and stir over high heat until sauce thickens.

Add linguine and toss well. Add peanuts and toss again. Turn into serving bowl and allow flavors to blend.

Serve at room temperature. Garnish with scallion brushes if desired.

Serves 6.

Hacked Chicken and Noodles in a Spicy Sauce

Once again our favorite peanut-sesame sauce that marries so well with chicken and noodles.

12 ounces vermicelli
1 pound boneless, skinless chicken breasts, poached and shredded
2 cucumbers, peeled, halved, seeded and cut into half-rounds

Sauce
½ teaspoon ground Szechuan peppercorns
1-inch piece of ginger, minced
2 cloves garlic, minced
2 scallions, minced
5 tablespoons soy sauce
2 tablespoons red wine vinegar
2 teaspoons sugar
2 tablespoons sesame oil
1 teaspoon hot chili oil
2 tablespoons water
¼ cup low-fat creamy peanut butter

Cook pasta until al dente, drain, rinse with cold water and drain again.

Mix all sauce ingredients together. If sauce is too thick, add water; if too thin, add more peanut butter.

In large bowl, toss pasta, cucumber, chicken and sauce. Let flavors blend. Serve at room temperature or chilled.

Serves 6.

Asian Chicken and Pasta with Fruit

*Y*ou *might use this salad as a side dish with jumbo shrimp grilled on the hibachi. Frosted bowls of lemon sherbet topped with candied ginger shreds and coconut make a refreshing dessert.*

8 ounces twist pasta
3 cups shredded cooked chicken
8-ounce can pineapple tidbits, drained
1 cup fresh seedless grapes
1 cup thinly sliced celery
½ cup thinly sliced water chestnuts
1 recipe Low-Fat Tarragon and Soy Vinaigrette (page 160)

Cook pasta until al dente, drain well and toss with ¼ cup of the Low-Fat Tarragon and Soy Vinaigrette. Chill.

Add chicken, pineapple, grapes, celery and water chestnuts to pasta. Add about ½ cup additional dressing and toss lightly. Chill about 1 hour before serving.

Serves 6.

Sesame Chicken and Twists Salad

A whole new taste treat. Sesame seed, not sesame oil, is used here. The effect is entirely different.

8 ounces twist pasta
1 pound boneless, skinless chicken breasts, poached, cut into ¼-inch strips
½ box frozen snow peas, thawed only
1 can water chestnuts, sliced
1 bunch scallions, sliced diagonally
2 tablespoons sesame seeds, lightly toasted
Salt and pepper to taste

Dressing
4 tablespoons dry sherry
1 tablespoon lemon juice
2 tablespoons Dijon mustard
2 tablespoons soy sauce
2 teaspoons sugar
1 teaspoon minced fresh ginger or ½ teaspoon ground
¼ cup olive or canola oil
¼ cup chicken broth, fat removed
Hot pepper sauce or red pepper flakes to taste

Cook pasta to al dente stage, drain, rinse with cold water and drain again.

In large bowl, gently but thoroughly toss pasta, chicken, snow peas, scallions, water chestnuts, sesame seeds. Add salt and pepper to taste.

To make dressing, mix well all dressing ingredients except oil and hot pepper. Gradually add oil to dressing, beating constantly until mixture is emulsified. Add hot pepper sauce or pepper flakes to taste.

Pour dressing over chicken and pasta mixture and toss well.

Serve chilled or at room temperature.

Serves 6.

Chicken, Green Pepper and Linguine, Oriental Style

This dish is good hot or warm, but we think it's best served chilled on large white plates with chopsticks.

12 ounces linguine
1 pound boneless, skinless chicken breasts, cut into thin strips
1 tablespoon cornstarch
4 large green peppers, cut into thin strips
1 bunch scallions, cut on the diagonal into 1-inch pieces
2-3 hot dried red peppers
1 teaspoon Szechuan peppercorns
2 tablespoons cornstarch

Dressing
6 tablespoons soy sauce
2 teaspoons sesame oil
2 tablespoons vinegar
2 tablespoons dry sherry or vermouth
Chicken broth, as needed

Cook linguine until al dente, drain, rinse with cold water and drain again.

Spray wok or large skillet with Pam and heat until quite hot. Stir-fry vegetables with hot dried peppers and peppercorns over high heat; remove from pan with slotted spoon. Shake chicken strips with cornstarch in bag; stir-fry 2-3 minutes or until lightly browned. Mix vegetables and chicken together.

Mix dressing ingredients except chicken broth together, pour over chicken and vegetables, and stir-fry about one minute. Add small amount of chicken broth if dry.

Add linguine and blend well. Serve at desired temperature.

Serves 6.

Chicken and Noodles in a Chinese Chili Paste Sauce

Intensely flavored Chinese chili paste with garlic adds a special zip to this salad. Serve with still-crisp stir-fried assorted vegetables — stir-fry in a non-stick pan coated with olive oil spray.

12 ounces linguine or thin spaghetti
4 boneless, skinless chicken breasts
1 medium onion stuck with 3 whole cloves
1 stalk celery, halved
1 bunch scallions, sliced on the diagonal into 1-inch pieces
3 cloves garlic, minced
1 tablespoon chopped fresh ginger
1 tablespoon dry sherry
4 tablespoons cold tea
4 tablespoons soy sauce
1½ teaspoons chili paste with garlic (available at Chinese groceries and gourmet shops)
2 teaspoons cornstarch
1 tablespoon olive or canola oil

Cook pasta until al dente, drain, rinse with cold water and drain again.

Poach chicken in water to cover, with onion and celery, for 15 minutes. Remove chicken and reserve broth.

Cut or tear chicken into thin strips and add to pasta.

In wok or skillet, briefly saute scallions, garlic and ginger in 1 tablespoon oil. Add sherry, cold tea, soy sauce, chili paste, cornstarch and ½ cup reserved broth. Cook over high heat about 1 minute.

Pour over pasta and chicken and toss well. Add by the spoonful more broth as necessary. Allow flavors to blend at least 2 hours before serving. Serve at room temperature or chilled.

Serves 6.

Layered Chicken and Pasta Salad

A *make-in-advance main dish that is nutritious as well as attractive. Serve in a clear glass bowl so that family or guests can enjoy the colorful layering.*

1½ cups macaroni or other tube pasta
2 cups cubed cooked chicken
1½ teaspoons curry powder
½ teaspoon salt
¼ teaspoon paprika
¼ teaspoon freshly ground pepper
2 cups shredded iceberg lettuce
2 cups shredded romaine lettuce
1 large cucumber, peeled, seeded and sliced
1 large green pepper, chopped (red pepper looks smashing if available)
4 green onions, chopped

Dressing
½ cup low-fat mayonnaise
½ cup fat-free yogurt
2 tablespoons lemon juice
1 teaspoon salt
¼ teaspoon freshly ground pepper
2 tablespoons chopped parsley, for garnish
2 tomatoes, cut in wedges, for garnish

Cook pasta until al dente, drain, rinse with cold water and drain again.

In medium bowl mix chicken with curry power, salt, paprika and pepper.

In a large clear bowl (about 4-quart size), layer iceberg and romaine lettuce, curried chicken, cucumber, macaroni, green pepper and onions.

Stir together mayonnaise, yogurt, lemon juice, salt and pepper.

Spread on top of layered ingredients. Cover tightly with plastic wrap and chill several hours or overnight.

Garnish with parsley and tomato wedges before serving. Toss at the table.

Serves 6.

Dilled Chicken and Linguine Salad

An excellent luncheon entree, served with sliced tomatoes and warm rolls. Kids will love this salad too.

12 ounces linguine or fettuccine
1 whole boneless, skinless chicken breast
4 medium dill pickles, chopped
4 stalks of celery, thinly sliced
6 green onions, chopped
2 tablespoons capers, rinsed and drained
12 small pimento-stuffed olives
2 egg whites, chopped

Dressing
$\frac{1}{2}$ cup low-fat sour cream or fat-free yogurt
$\frac{1}{4}$ cup chicken broth
Juice of 1 lemon
$\frac{1}{2}$ teaspoon dillweed or 2 teaspoons fresh dill, chopped
1 teaspoon salt
$\frac{1}{2}$ teaspoon freshly ground pepper

Barely cover the chicken breast with water and add 1 teaspoon salt, 1 small onion, 2 whole cloves and 4 peppercorns. Simmer 15 minutes. Remove from broth and cool. Shred meat coarsely. Reserve broth.

While chicken is simmering, cook pasta until al dente, drain, rinse with cold water and drain again.

Mix dressing ingredients together in a small bowl. Gently mix the pasta, chicken, celery, onions and capers and about $\frac{2}{3}$ of the dressing. Add more dressing as needed. Refrigerate if not serving immediately. Mound the mixture on a lettuce-lined platter and garnish with the olives and chopped egg whites.

Serves 6.

Green Noodles with Mushrooms and Chicken

A lovely contrast of colors as well as taste. Add the sliced mushrooms just before serving for extra freshness.

12 ounces green fettuccine
1 whole boneless, skinless chicken breast
1/2 pound sliced mushrooms
1 cup coarsely chopped seeded tomatoes
1/2 cup chopped green onion tops
1/4 cup chopped parsley
Fresh basil leaves or oregano for garnish

Dressing
1/4 cup low-fat mayonnaise
1/4 cup chicken broth
1 teaspoon Italian seasonings
1/2 teaspoon salt
1/4 teaspoon freshly ground pepper

Cook fettuccine until al dente, drain, rinse with cold water and drain again.

Poach chicken breast in seasoned, simmering water until just done, about 15 minutes; cool.

Dice the chicken and add to the pasta.

Mix the dressing ingredients and add to the pasta along with the chopped tomatoes and onion tops. Refrigerate until serving time.

Sprinkle the sliced mushrooms and fresh herbs on top just before serving and toss at the table.

Serves 6.

Rotelle and Chicken Salad

Any type of cooked left-over chicken, even from Sunday's barbecue, is suitable for this melange of red, white and green salad ingredients.

12 ounces rotelle
2 cups shredded or cubed cooked chicken
2 cups broccoli florets
1 large green or red sweet pepper, thinly sliced
½ box cherry tomatoes, halved if large
½ cup sliced mushrooms
3 tablespoons toasted slivered almonds or toasted sunflower seeds
½ cup Low-Fat Creamy Dressing (page 171) or ½ cup Low-Fat Herbed Vinaigrette (page 157)
¼ cup chopped parsley

Cook pasta until al dente, drain, rinse with cold water and drain again.

Plunge broccoli florets into pan of boiling water for 1 minute, then rinse with cold water and drain thoroughly. Add chicken, vegetables and nuts to pasta with dressing of your choice. Mix thoroughly and taste for salt and pepper. Sprinkle with chopped parsley and serve at room temperature or lightly chilled.

Serves 6.

Chicken and Snow Peas with Fruit and Pasta

Serve this refreshing and unusual combination on a torrid summer evening to your weekend guests.

8 ounces spaghetti or fusilli
1 whole boneless, skinless chicken breast
3 tablespoons olive oil
Salt and pepper to taste
5 or 6 nectarines, depending on size, pitted and sliced
4 red plums, pitted and sliced
1/4 pound snow peas or sugar snap peas, or 1/2 10-ounce box frozen snow peas, thawed
6 green onions, sliced
3 tablespoons walnuts, coarsely chopped

Dressing
2 tablespoons walnut or sesame oil
1/4 cup olive or canola oil
1/4 cup white wine vinegar
2 tablespoons minced fresh rosemary or 1 teaspoon dried rosemary, crushed
1 teaspoon salt or more to taste
1/2 teaspoon freshly ground black pepper

Mix dressing before preparing other ingredients. Set aside; do not refrigerate.

Cook pasta until al dente, drain, rinse with cold water and drain again. Toss with 2 tablespoons dressing. Do not refrigerate.

Saute chicken breast in the oil until opaque and firm to the touch; do not brown. Cool, slice into thin strips.

Pour boiling water over pea pods; do not cook.

Combine chicken, nectarines, plums, snow peas or sugar snap peas, onions and walnuts. Toss gently with remaining dressing. Chill.

At serving time add chicken mixture to pasta and toss thoroughly but gently.

Serves 6.

Chicken and Mango Chutney Salad

The subtle flavors of India have made this salad a favorite. A selection of Indian breads, and cardamom-flavored peach sherbet for dessert, make a light lunch or late supper.

12 ounces rotelle or fusilli
2 cups cooked and shredded chicken
$2/3$ cup thinly sliced celery
1 cup red seedless grapes, halved
$1/4$ cup chopped green pepper
$1/4$ cup toasted sliced almonds
Extra whole red grapes for garnish

Dressing
$1/2$ cup mango chutney or other type chutney, large fruit pieces chopped
1 cup low-fat sour cream
$1 1/2$ teaspoons freshly grated ginger
1 tablespoon honey
$1/2$ teaspoon salt
1 teaspoon curry powder, or more to taste

Mix dressing before preparing other ingredients. Set aside; do not refrigerate.

Cook the pasta until al dente, drain, rinse with cold water and drain again. Gently mix pasta with shredded chicken and $3/4$ cup dressing. Allow flavors to blend. Add vegetables, grapes and almonds to pasta and chicken. Refrigerate until $1/2$ hour before serving.

Before serving, taste for seasonings, drizzle with remaining dressing and garnish with whole grapes.

Serves 6.

Vermicelli and Chicken Salad with Lemon Dressing

*T*angy but light with a Far East appeal.

8 ounces vermicelli
1 pound boneless, skinless chicken breasts
1 small onion stuck with 3 whole cloves
1 carrot, sliced
1 stalk celery, with leaves
1 clove garlic
2 teaspoons salt
6 peppercorns
2 cups fresh bean sprouts, rinsed in boiling water and drained
1 cup bamboo shoots, julienned

Dressing
3/4 cup reserved broth
1 tablespoon sugar
1 tablespoon soy sauce
1/4 cup lemon juice or more to taste
1 teaspoon cornstarch
2 teaspoons cold water
1 teaspoon grated lemon rind
White pepper to taste

Garnish
3 green onions, cut into 1-inch pieces, then slivered vertically
2 lemons, halved, seeded and very thinly sliced

Combine the chicken with water to cover, onion, carrot, celery, garlic clove, salt and peppercorns. Bring to a boil, reduce heat, and simmer until just tender.

Remove chicken, strain broth and reserve. Shred chicken when cool.

Cook vermicelli until al dente, drain, rinse under cold water and drain again.

Mix the cornstarch with the cold water and add to the other dressing ingredients in a small saucepan. Simmer until slightly thickened; set aside to cool.

In a large shallow bowl toss the vermicelli, chicken, bean sprouts, bamboo shoots and dressing. Sprinkle slivered green onions on top and surround with the lemon slices.

Serves 6.

Orzo and Poultry Salad

Delicate rice-shaped pasta teams up with yesterday's left-over chicken or turkey. For a winter treat, substitute anise-flavored fennel for sliced celery.

1½ cups orzo
2 cups shredded cooked chicken or turkey
1 cup chopped green onions (use tops and bottoms)
1 cup sliced celery or the stem part of a fennel bulb
¼ cup chopped parsley

Dressing
½ cup low-fat mayonnaise
¼ cup chicken broth
1 teaspoon salt
½ pepper
2 tablespoons tarragon vinegar
½ teaspoon tarragon, crushed

Cook pasta until al dente, drain, rinse with cold water and drain again.

Blend dressing ingredients in a serving bowl. Add the pasta and remaining ingredients and toss gently but thoroughly. Taste for seasonings and chill until serving time.

Serves 6.

Creamy and Curried Chicken, Apple and Fusilli Salad

Serve this main-course curried salad with a zesty chutney and some interesting Indian breads such as puri or chappati.

12 ounces fusilli
1 whole boneless, skinless chicken breast
3 medium red apples, unpeeled and diced
$\frac{1}{2}$ cup raisins
1 cup chopped celery
$\frac{1}{2}$ cup sliced ripe olives
$\frac{1}{2}$ cup green onion, tops only, sliced 1 inch long
3 tablespoons slivered almonds

Dressing
$\frac{1}{2}$ cup low-fat mayonnaise
2 tablespoons skim milk
2 teaspoons curry powder, or more to taste
$1\frac{1}{2}$ teaspoons salt
$\frac{1}{8}$ teaspoon cayenne
1 tablespoon lemon juice

Cook pasta until al dente, drain, rinse with cold water and drain again.

Poach chicken breast with a small onion stuck with 2 whole cloves, 4 peppercorns, a small stalk of celery and 1 teaspoon salt. Simmer gently just until firm to the touch. Cool and shred. (Save broth for a cold soup base.) Cover chicken with plastic wrap and refrigerate.

Blend dressing ingredients in a small bowl.

Add the chicken, apples, raisins, celery, olives, green onions and almonds to the pasta. Pour the dressing over the pasta mixture and toss lightly but well.

Cover and refrigerate at least one hour.

Serves 6.

Pasta with Duck
and Peach Preserve Dressing

*T*his is an elegant warm-weather entree or first course.

8 ounces rotini or other spiral pasta
1 whole duck breast, skin removed
3 tablespoons roasted and coarsely chopped pecans
1 leek, sliced lengthwise and then thinly sliced to make $^2/_3$ cup
$^2/_3$ cup sliced celery
2 teaspoons chopped fresh rosemary, or $^1/_2$ teaspoon dried rosemary, crushed
1 fresh peach for garnish

Dressing
$^1/_2$ cup low-fat mayonnaise
$^1/_2$ cup peach preserves
2 tablespoons walnut or olive oil
$^1/_4$ cup peach or other fruit-flavored vinegar
1 teaspoon salt
$^1/_2$ teaspoon freshly ground pepper

Simmer the duck breast in water flavored with rosemary, basil, thyme, oregano, salt and peppercorns just until it becomes firm to the touch. Cool and then pull or slice meat into thin strips.

Cook pasta until al dente, drain, rinse with cold water and drain again.

Toss pasta and duck with pecans, leeks, celery and rosemary. Mix dressing ingredients and blend gently with pasta salad.

Lightly chill before serving. Garnish with fresh peach slices that have been brushed with lemon juice to prevent browning.

Serves 6.

Turkey with Ginger and Linguine

*T*urn *left-over holiday turkey into an Asian surprise. To start, serve won ton soup from your local Chinese carry-out. For fun, end with fortune cookies.*

8 ounces linguine or tagliatelle pasta
2 cups turkey meat cut into strips
2 cups cooked peas (fresh or frozen)
½ cup chopped green onions
3 tablespoons slivered or sliced almonds, toasted
¼ cup chopped red pepper or 3 tablespoons chopped pimento

Dressing
¼ cup olive or canola oil
3 tablespoons tarragon vinegar
1 tablespoon Dijon mustard
2 tablespoons broth or water
2 teaspoons freshly grated ginger
1 teaspoon salt
¼ teaspoon freshly ground pepper

Cook pasta until al dente, drain, rinse with cold water and drain again. Place in a large serving bowl.

In a medium bowl mix the dressing ingredients. Add ¼ cup to the pasta and toss gently.

To the remaining dressing add the turkey, peas, onions, almonds and red pepper or pimento. Mix thoroughly but carefully. Put on top of the pasta and refrigerate until ½ hour before serving.

Toss at the table.

Serves 6.

Turkey and Asparagus Pasta Salad

Left-over turkey will rise to new heights with this palate- and eye-pleasing salad.

12 ounces bow-tie or farfalle pasta
24 small, very thin slices of turkey
1 pound asparagus
4 tomatoes, peeled and thinly sliced
½ bunch watercress, coarse stems removed

Dressing
½ cup fat-free yogurt or low-fat sour cream
¼ cup low-fat ricotta cheese
¼ cup vegetable broth
2 tablespoons basil or white wine vinegar
1 clove garlic, minced
10 fresh basil leaves, coarsely chopped
1 tablespoon finely chopped celery leaves
½ teaspoon sugar
1 teaspoon salt
¼ teaspoon freshly ground pepper

Thoroughly mix the dressing but do not make it smooth. Taste for seasonings.

Cook pasta until al dente, drain, rinse under cold water and drain again. Toss with ¼ cup of the dressing.

Wash asparagus, break off woody ends and peel if you wish; cut into 1-inch lengths. Simmer for about 3 minutes and drain.

Tear watercress into bite-size pieces.

Combine the sliced turkey, tomatoes, asparagus and watercress. Refrigerate until serving time.

At serving time arrange the pasta in a shallow bowl or deep platter. Place the turkey mixture on top and drizzle the remaining dressing over all.

Serves 6.

Main Course Pasta "Club" Salad

This main course salad uses everyone's favorite sandwich ingredients to provide a refreshing alternative to the usual sandwich-type meal. Round out the menu with a green vegetable, cooked crisp-tender, a fruit-flavored spritzer and assorted melon wedges for dessert.

12 ounces rotini
2 cups cooked chicken or turkey, cubed
3 tablespoons bacon bits
2 ripe tomatoes, cut in small pieces, or $1/2$ box cherry tomatoes, cut in half if large
2 cups iceberg lettuce, cut in $1/4$-inch slices
$1/4$ cup low-fat Swiss cheese, julienned
Salt and freshly ground pepper, to taste

Dressing
$1/2$ cup low-fat mayonnaise
$1/4$ cup vegetable broth
1 tablespoon white wine vinegar
1 tablespoon lemon juice
$1/2$ teaspoon tarragon, crushed

Cook rotini until al dente, drain, rinse with cold water and drain again.

Blend dressing ingredients until smooth. Mix dressing, rotini, chicken and bacon bits together, and refrigerate at least 1 hour so flavors can blend. Just before serving, toss with the tomatoes, lettuce and Swiss cheese. Add salt and freshly ground pepper to taste.

Serves 6.

Turkey Tetrazzini Salad

We've given an old standby a new twist. The recipe can easily be doubled or tripled for a buffet supper or a Little League picnic.

12 ounces linguine, broken into thirds
2 cups cooked turkey, cubed
$\frac{1}{2}$ pound fresh mushrooms, thinly sliced
$\frac{1}{2}$ box tiny frozen peas, thawed only
1 small jar diced pimentos, drained
$\frac{1}{4}$ cup sliced almonds, toasted
Salt and freshly ground pepper to taste

Dressing
$\frac{1}{2}$ cup low-fat cottage cheese
$\frac{1}{4}$ cup skim milk
2 tablespoons lemon juice
1 tablespoon Worcestershire sauce
$\frac{1}{2}$ teaspoon thyme, crushed
Tabasco sauce to taste

Cook linguine until al dente, drain, rinse with cold water and drain again.

Whirl first five dressing ingredients in a blender or food processor until smooth. Add Tabasco drop by drop to taste; dressing should have a little zip to it.

Combine linguine, turkey, mushrooms, peas, pimentos and almonds in a large bowl. Add dressing, toss well and refrigerate at least 1 hour. Just before serving add salt and pepper to taste and toss again.

Serves 6.

Pasta Salads with Meat

Pasta Salads with Meat

Small quantities of meat, including leftovers, can be combined with pasta and vegetables to make a delicious meal.

Our approach with these recipes is to use the meat sparingly, trimmed of fat and often chopped more finely. This allows you to enjoy the flavor, but with less fat — and no sense of deprivation.

Pasta Deli Salad

*W*hat could be simpler than one stop at the deli counter and another at the produce department, then cooking up a pot of pasta?

10 ounces twist, shell or penne pasta
2 ounces hard salami, cut into thin strips
4 ounces low-fat provolone cheese, cut into thin strips
2 ounces jarred marinated mushrooms
1 small red onion, cut into thin rings
1 cup chopped red or green pepper (or try sliced pimentos for a change)
12 black olives, pitted and sliced
1/4 cup chopped parsley

Dressing
1/4 cup canola oil
2 tablespoons red wine vinegar, or more to taste
1 teaspoon Dijon mustard
1/2 teaspoon oregano, crushed
1/2 teaspoon celery seed
1/2 teaspoon salt, or to taste
Freshly ground pepper to taste

Mix all dressing ingredients thoroughly in a medium bowl. Cook pasta until al dente and drain. Toss in a large bowl with 2 tablespoons dressing. Do not refrigerate.

Add salami, cheese, mushrooms, onion, pepper, olives and parsley to remaining dressing and toss well.

Combine the deli ingredients with the pasta and toss together. Serve at room temperature or lightly chilled if the day is hot.

Serves 6.

Antipasto Salad Platter

*T*his colorful salad is the perfect way to begin an Italian-style meal. The main course might be a crispy chicken roasted with lemon: Slice one lemon, add to chicken cavity with two cloves of garlic; rub bird with olive oil and salt and pepper; roast at 400 degrees until well browned. Make a sauce of the pan juices, juice from the lemon slices, and a little white wine and/or chicken broth; cook down until syrupy. Makes about 1 tablespoon sauce for each serving of chicken. Serve with Italian bread and a light red wine.

10 ounces small shells or other small pasta
2 green or red bell peppers, diced
½ pound mushrooms, sliced
2 ounces low-fat provolone cheese, shredded
1 16-ounce can chick peas (garbanzo beans), rinsed and drained
2 ounces salami, cut in thin strips
12 Greek olives, pitted
1 tin anchovy fillets, drained

Dressing
⅓ cup canola oil
3 tablespoons fresh lemon juice
1 teaspoon salt
¼ teaspoon freshly ground pepper
⅛ teaspoon red pepper flakes, or Tabasco sauce to taste
1 clove garlic, crushed
1 teaspoon basil leaves, crushed, or 1 tablespoon fresh basil, chopped

Cook pasta until al dente, drain, rinse with cold water and drain again. In a small bowl thoroughly blend dressing ingredients, then mix with pasta in a large bowl. Cool, then toss with remaining ingredients. Cover and refrigerate for at least one hour. Adjust seasoning if necessary and toss again before serving.

Serves 6.

Pepperoni and Shell Salad

*I*talian bread and an attractive platter of assorted melon wedges and other fruits are all you need to serve with this salad for a luncheon or light supper for family or friends.

10 ounces small shell pasta
1 14-ounce can artichoke hearts
2 or 3 bell peppers, preferably red but green are fine
1½ cups broccoli florets
2 ounces thinly sliced pepperoni
3 tablespoons diced pimentos
2 tablespoons chopped Italian or regular parsley

Dressing
½ cup low-fat mayonnaise
¼ cup vegetable or chicken broth
2 tablespoons red wine vinegar, or more to taste
½ teaspoon salt
¼ teaspoon freshly ground pepper
1 tablespoon chopped fresh basil leaves, or 1 teaspoon dried basil, crushed
½ teaspoon oregano, crushed
1 tablespoon chopped Italian or regular parsley

Cook pasta until al dente, drain, rinse with cold water and drain again. Mix dressing in a large serving bowl, add pasta and toss.

Drain and quarter artichoke hearts. Seed and thinly slice peppers. Steam broccoli florets 2 minutes and rinse with cold water; drain well and pat dry with paper towels. Stack pepperoni slices and cut into thin strips.

Toss all the above ingredients with the dressing and adjust seasoning to taste. Serve chilled.

Serves 6.

Colorful Vegetables and Pasta with Pancetta

*T*his salad is always a knockout on buffet tables. Pancetta is similar to bacon but cured, not smoked, and is round and tightly packed like salami. Worth looking for at the Italian grocery. For an even lower fat version of this salad, bacon bits can be substituted.

10 ounces dried gnocchi or cavatelle
1 cup broccoli florets
1 cup cauliflower florets
1 cup quartered mushrooms
½ cup green onion, cut into ½-inch pieces
12 pitted ripe olives, sliced
2 ounces pancetta, sliced ¼ inch thick and julienned, or ¼ cup bacon bits
½ avocado, peeled and diced
1 large, ripe tomato, seeded and chopped, or 12 cherry tomatoes, left whole if small
1 recipe Low-Fat Herbed Vinaigrette (page 157)

Cook pasta until al dente, drain, rinse with cold water and drain again. Blanch broccoli and cauliflower for 2 minutes, drain, rinse with cold water and drain again. Pat dry with paper towels. Add to pasta in a large serving bowl and toss lightly. Cover and refrigerate.

Mix ½ cup of the Low-Fat Herbed Vinaigrette dressing with the mushrooms, green onions and olives and marinate at least 1 hour, covered and refrigerated.

Just before serving add pancetta and marinated vegetables to the pasta, toss with remaining dressing and adjust seasoning if necessary. Add avocado and tomato and toss again, very gently.

Serves 6.

Penne and Beans a la Tuscany

This variation of the better-known Tuna, Bean and Pasta salad makes a wonderful luncheon dish or addition to an antipasto platter.

10 ounces penne or other short tube pasta
3 ounces hard salami, thinly sliced and julienned
1 16-ounce can chick peas (garbanzo beans), rinsed and drained
1 medium red onion, thinly sliced
¼ cup capers, rinsed and drained
1 cup chopped parsley, preferably the flat-leaved variety
12 ripe olives, with pits

Dressing
4 tablespoons olive oil
2 tablespoons red wine vinegar
2 tablespoons vegetable or chicken broth
2 cloves garlic, minced
½ teaspoon salt
½ teaspoon freshly ground pepper
½ teaspoon thyme, crushed

Whisk dressing ingredients in a small bowl. Set aside.

Cook pasta until al dente, drain and transfer to a serving bowl. Toss with ¼ cup dressing.

Add salami to pasta with beans, onion, capers, parsley and olives. Add remaining dressing and toss again; adjust seasoning as necessary. Do not chill; serve at room temperature.

Serves 6.

Rotelle, Ham and Fontina Cheese Salad

*H*ere *is an alternative to your favorite ham and cheese sandwich. More crunch, fewer calories.*

10 ounces rotelle or other twist pasta
1 cup ham (leftover is best), trimmed of all fat and julienned
¼ pound low-fat fontina or Swiss cheese, coarsely grated
2 cups red cabbage, finely shredded
3 tablespoons coarsely chopped walnuts, toasted

Dressing
¼ cup white wine
2 tablespoons white wine vinegar
3 tablespoons chopped green onions
1 clove garlic, minced
1 tablespoon Dijon mustard
½ teaspoon salt
¼ teaspoon freshly ground pepper
¼ cup olive oil
¼ cup minced parsley

Cook pasta until al dente, drain, rinse with cold water, and drain again. Mix dressing ingredients. In a large bowl, toss pasta with ¼ cup of the dressing. Cover and cool to room temperature.

Mix the ham and cheese with ¼ cup dressing, cover and chill.

Toss cabbage with remaining dressing, cover and chill.

Shortly before serving, toss together the pasta and the ham, cheese and cabbage mixtures. Sprinkle with the chopped walnuts and serve.

Serves 6.

Touch of Spring Vermicelli Salad

*W*hat *a nice way to celebrate the first asparagus of spring and enjoy* leftover Easter ham.

12 ounces vermicelli or thin spaghetti
½ pound fresh asparagus, ends snapped off and stems cut into 1-inch pieces
1 cup ham slivers
1 small red onion, halved and thinly sliced
¼ cup canola or olive oil, divided
2 tablespoons vegetable or chicken broth
1 teaspoon salt, divided
½ teaspoon freshly ground pepper
½ teaspoon marjoram, crushed
3 tablespoons chopped parsley

Cook vermicelli until al dente, drain and rinse with cold water and drain again. Toss with 1 tablespoon oil.

Heat 1 tablespoon oil in skillet; add asparagus, onions, ½ teaspoon salt and marjoram and toss to coat. Add broth and stir- fry until tender but crisp.

Add vegetables, ham, remaining oil, ground pepper and parsley to pasta and toss gently. Add remaining salt to taste. Serve at room temperature.

Serves 6.

Layered Pasta Salad

*P*repare this salad, a contrast of color and taste, in advance to
accommodate a busy schedule.

2 cups elbow or shell pasta
2 cups shredded iceberg lettuce
1 cup julienne strips of ham, all fat removed
2 hard-cooked egg whites, chopped
½ 10-ounce package frozen tiny green peas, thawed
½ cup shredded low-fat Monterey Jack cheese
Salt and freshly ground pepper

Dressing
¼ cup low-fat mayonnaise
¼ cup low-fat sour cream or fat-free yogurt
2 teaspoons Dijon mustard
¼ cup chopped green onion
½ teaspoon basil leaves, crushed
½ teaspoon salt
¼ teaspoon freshly ground pepper
2 tablespoons chopped parsley, for garnish

Cook pasta until al dente, drain, rinse with cold water and drain again. Set
aside to cool or refrigerate.

Combine the mayonnaise, sour cream or yogurt, mustard, green onion,
basil and salt and pepper in a small bowl. Set aside.

In a 3-quart bowl, preferably glass, layer the lettuce and top with the
cooled pasta. Next layer the egg whites and sprinkle with salt and pepper.
Add in layers the ham, thawed peas and shredded cheese. Spread the
dressing mixture carefully over the top and to the edge of the bowl.
Cover with plastic wrap and refrigerate at least overnight. Sprinkle with
chopped parsley before serving. Toss at the table.

Serves 6.

Pasta and Ham Picnic Salad

*F*or a casual look and an easy cleanup, serve this old-fashioned picnic
salad in a foil-lined basket. Remember to keep salad well chilled until
serving time.

10 ounces rigatoni or elbow pasta
½ pound cooked ham steak, trimmed of fat and julienned into 1½-inch lengths
2 red or green peppers, diced
1 medium red onion, diced
10 small sweet pickles, sliced
½ box cherry tomatoes, halved
1 hard-cooked egg white, chopped
2 tablespoons chopped fresh dillweed

Dressing
¼ cup low-fat mayonnaise
¼ cup fat-free yogurt
2 teaspoons dry au jus gravy mix (powdered bouillon can be substituted)
2 tablespoons pickle juice
1 tablespoon vinegar
Salt and freshly ground pepper to taste
1-2 cloves garlic, minced

Cook pasta until al dente, drain, rinse with cold water and drain again.
Mix dressing ingredients in a small bowl.

In a large bowl mix together pasta, ham, peppers, onion, pickles,
tomatoes and egg white. Add dressing and mix thoroughly. Sprinkle
chopped dill on top and refrigerate until serving time. Toss again before
serving.

Serves 6.

Rotelle with Beef and Mushrooms

*T*his is especially nice when the steak is grilled to medium rare on the outdoor grill and home-grown tomatoes are at their peak. Flank steak is a very lean cut of beef.

10 ounces rotelle or other twist-type pasta
1 small flank steak, grilled and thinly sliced (about 2 cups)
½ pound mushrooms, thinly sliced
3 dill pickles, sliced
2 tomatoes, cut into thin wedges for garnish

Dressing
¼ cup olive or canola oil
2 tablespoons red wine vinegar
2 tablespoons capers, rinsed, drained and minced if large
2 teaspoons Dijon mustard
2 tablespoons minced parsley
½ teaspoon tarragon, crushed or 2 teaspoons minced fresh tarragon leaves
½ teaspoon salt
Freshly ground pepper to taste

Mix the dressing ingredients and pour over the prepared sliced meat and mushrooms. Cover and marinate about two hours, refrigerated.

Meanwhile, cook the pasta until al dente, drain, rinse with cold water and drain again. Turn into a large bowl and cool to room temperature.

Shortly before serving, add the marinated meat, mushrooms and pickles to the pasta and toss. Garnish with tomato wedges.

Serves 6.

Beef, Snow Peas and Bow Tie Pasta with Bleu Cheese Dressing

A casual Sunday night supper might include this satisfying salad. During the summer try substituting fresh sugar snap peas for snow peas. In a hurry? Use deli roast beef, trimmed of fat, and frozen snow peas.

10 ounces bow tie (farfalle) pasta
½ pound rare roast beef, trimmed of any fat and cut into thin strips
½ pound mushrooms, thinly sliced
¼ pound fresh snow peas, tipped, or ½ box frozen snow peas, thawed and patted dry
½ bunch watercress, heavy stems removed

Dressing
½ cup low-fat sour cream or fat-free yogurt
¼ cup low-fat Bleu cheese, crumbled
2 tablespoons skim milk
4 tablespoons red wine or herb vinegar
2 green onions, finely chopped
½ teaspoon marjoram or basil, crushed
¼ teaspoon thyme, crushed
½ teaspoon salt
¼ teaspoon freshly ground pepper, or more to taste

Cook pasta until al dente, drain, rinse with cold water and drain again.

Drop fresh snow peas or sugar snap peas into boiling water and cook 1 minute. Drain and rinse with cold water and drain again. Pat dry, then cut in half, cover and chill.

Mix dressing ingredients in blender or food processor until just blended but not smooth. Cover and chill.

On a large shallow bowl or platter, arrange the pasta and spoon some dressing over it. Starting at the outer edge of the platter, make a ring of watercress on top of the pasta, then rings of the mushrooms and snow peas; mound the beef in the center. Drizzle each ring with dressing. Serve chilled.

Serves 6.

Piquant Beef, Cherry Tomato and Pasta Salad

*S*ave some of last night's roast beef or grill a small flank steak (very low in fat) for this satisfying salad. Precede the salad with a cold carrot or zucchini soup. If there's a bit of a nip in the air, serve a hot soup.

10 ounces rotelle or shell pasta
2 cups cubed rare roast beef or steak
18 cherry tomatoes, halved if large
1 cup chopped green onions
⅓ cup chopped parsley
¼ cup capers, rinsed and drained
10 or 12 fresh basil leaves, torn, or 2 teaspoons dried basil, crushed
12 cured black olives

Dressing
¼ cup canola or olive oil
¼ cup beef broth
3 tablespoons red wine or herb vinegar
2-ounce tin anchovy fillets, drained
3 cloves garlic, chopped
½ teaspoon salt
½ teaspoon freshly ground pepper

Cook pasta until al dente, drain, rinse with cold water and drain again. Transfer to a large bowl, cover and cool.

If you are using a food processor, add to it all the dressing ingredients and combine until well mixed. Or mash the anchovy fillets with a fork, then add the other dressing ingredients and whisk together until well blended.

To the pasta add the cubed beef, green onions, parsley, capers and basil and toss. Add the tomatoes, olives and dressing and toss again, gently.

Serves 6.

Beef and Pasta with Broccoli and Asparagus

A *natural when asparagus is at its peak — and its cheapest. What a treat, though, to serve in mid-winter when some California spears manage to slip into the supermarkets. Start with a hot soup, accompany with hot herbed rolls and you won't notice the cold outside.*

10 ounces fettuccine, or bucatini if available
1 small flank steak
½ bunch broccoli, about ¾ pound
1 pound fresh asparagus

Dressing
¼ cup olive or canola oil, divided
¼ cup soy sauce
¼ cup vegetable or beef broth
2 tablespoons sesame oil
1-inch piece fresh ginger, peeled and grated
2 cloves garlic, minced
1 tablespoon minced onion
½ teaspoon freshly ground pepper, or to taste
1 teaspoon sugar

Broil flank steak to medium rare or quickly pan-fry. Cool and slice thinly.

Cook pasta until al dente, drain, rinse with cold water and drain again. Toss with 1 tablespoon oil.

Remove the stalks from the broccoli and save for another use. Break the florets into bite-size pieces. Break off the woody ends of the asparagus and wash well. Slice on the diagonal into 1-inch pieces.

Blanch the broccoli for 30 seconds in boiling water and remove with a slotted spoon to a bowl of ice water. Add the asparagus to the boiling water and blanch for 30 seconds. Remove with a slotted spoon to the ice water. Drain well and pat dry with paper towels.

Combine the dressing ingredients and whisk until well mixed.

Toss the beef with some of the dressing and marinate briefly. Put the pasta, meat and vegetables into an attractive bowl and toss with the remaining dressing. Serve at room temperature or lightly chilled.

Serves 6.

Corned Beef, Crunchy Cabbage and Pasta

This salad will draw raves at your next potluck supper.

10 ounces rotini or other twist pasta
1½ cups shredded cooked corned beef, obvious fat removed
1½ cups finely shredded cabbage
½ cup shredded carrots
½ cup thinly sliced celery
¼ cup chopped green pepper
½ cup chopped green onions
1 recipe Low-Fat Creamy Garlic Dressing (page 166)

Cook pasta until al dente, drain, rinse with cold water and drain again. Mix with ¼ cup of the Low-Fat Creamy Garlic Dressing and chill.

Prepare corned beef, cabbage, carrots, celery, green pepper and onions. Add to pasta and toss gently. Add remaining dressing and mix thoroughly. Chill before serving.

Serves 6.

Rotelle with Cabbage and Beef

A tasty main-dish salad. Serve it with dark bread and a bright vegetable — such as sliced tomatoes or curried vinaigrette carrots.

8 ounces rotelle or any twist pasta
½ pound cabbage, finely shredded
2 cups left-over pot roast (obvious fat removed), shredded
1 tablespoon olive or canola oil
2 teaspoons caraway seeds
Salt and freshly ground pepper to taste

Dressing
¼ cup olive oil
2 tablespoons red wine vinegar
½ teaspoon thyme, crushed
¼ teaspoon salt
½ teaspoon sugar

Cook pasta until al dente, drain, rinse with cold water and drain again.

Heat 1 tablespoon oil in skillet, add beef and fry until edges are crisp. Remove from heat and toss with cabbage, caraway seeds and salt and pepper.

Blend dressing ingredients in a small bowl.

Mix meat and cabbage mixture with pasta, add dressing and toss thoroughly. Serve warm or at room temperature.

Serves 6.

Lamb, Green Bean
and Orzo Salad

*P*lan ahead: *Buy a slightly heavier leg of lamb for dinner and enjoy this quick and tasty salad a few days later.*

1½ cups orzo or other tiny pasta
2 cups slivers of cooked lamb (obvious fat removed)
½ pound green beans, cut into 1-inch pieces
1 small red onion, finely chopped
1 red or green pepper, sliced in thin strips
¼ cup finely chopped parsley
Salt and freshly ground pepper to taste

Dressing
¼ cup olive or canola oil
¼ cup beef broth
3 tablespoons Dijon mustard
2 teaspoons lemon juice
2 cloves garlic, minced
1 teaspoon dried rosemary, crushed, or 2 teaspoons fresh rosemary, chopped

Cook pasta until al dente, drain, rinse with cold water and drain again.

Blanch the beans for 1 minute in boiling water and remove with a slotted spoon to a bowl of ice water. Drain and pat dry with paper towels.

Mix dressing ingredients in a large attractive serving bowl and add the pasta, lamb, green beans, onion, sliced pepper and parsley. Mix thoroughly. Chill before serving.

Serves 6.

Lamb or Beef with Wheels or Shells

*T*his hearty salad is a "meal in itself," as Mother used to say. Serve with crunchy breadsticks or a good sourdough.

10 ounces wheels, shells or other pasta shape
2 cups julienned cooked lamb or beef, rare if possible (obvious fat removed)
1 small onion, finely grated
½ cup chopped parsley
2 red or green peppers, diced
2 stalks celery
2 medium cucumbers, peeled, seeded and sliced
2 large tomatoes, seeded and coarsely chopped
12 cured black olives
Mint leaves coarsely chopped, for garnish (optional)

Dressing
⅓ cup olive or canola oil
⅓ cup vegetable or beef broth
2 tablespoons lemon juice
2 tablespoons Dijon mustard
3 cloves garlic, minced
2 tablespoons capers, drained and rinsed, chopped if large
2 tablespoons chopped parsley
½ teaspoon dried rosemary, crushed
½ teaspoon thyme, crushed
½ teaspoon salt, or to taste
½ teaspoon freshly ground pepper
Grated peel of ½ lemon

Cook pasta until al dente, drain, rinse with cold water and drain again.

Mix dressing ingredients and marinate the julienned meat in ½ cup of the dressing for at least one hour.

Prepare all the vegetables and mix with the pasta in a large bowl.

At serving time, toss with the remaining dressing and transfer to a shallow serving bowl or platter. Surround the edge of the bowl with the meat and serve.

Serves 6.

Italian Sausage and Vegetables with Wheels

*T*his is a well-rounded nutritious salad that needs only fresh Italian bread to make a complete lunch. A bit of dessert would be nice too.

10 ounces wheels or elbow pasta
½ pound sweet (mild) Italian sausage, or Italian-flavored low-fat turkey or veal sausage
2 medium zucchini, scrubbed and thinly sliced
1 cup chopped green pepper, or a mixture of green and red
½ cup chopped pimentos
12 cured black olives

Dressing
¼ cup olive oil
2 tablespoons red wine vinegar
1 teaspoon Dijon mustard
2 cloves garlic, minced
½ teaspoon salt, or more to taste
¼ teaspoon freshly ground pepper
1 teaspoon basil, crushed

Cook pasta until al dente, drain, rinse with cold water and drain again. Transfer to a serving bowl.

Put sausage into a non-stick skillet and barely cover with water. Bring to a boil, then simmer for 20 minutes. Drain off water and lightly brown sausages. Cool sausages, slice thinly and add to the pasta.

To the bowl add the prepared zucchini, peppers, pimentos and olives. Pour the dressing over the pasta salad and toss. Serve at room temperature.

Serves 6.

Shells, Sausage and Peppers

Perfect family main course, quick and easy to fix. If good fresh green peppers are not available, you might try frozen chopped peppers. Also, add chunks of fresh tomatoes when they are in season; don't bother with the pale winter variety.

10 ounces shell pasta
1 pound sweet (mild) Italian sausage, or turkey or veal sausages with Italian seasonings
Olive oil spray
3 peppers, mixed red and green, coarsely chopped
3 cloves garlic, minced
¾ cup dry white wine or dry vermouth
¼ cup chicken broth
¼ cup chopped parsley
Salt and pepper to taste
3 fresh tomatoes (optional)

Cook pasta until al dente, drain, rinse with cold water and drain again.

Remove casing from sausages and break up sausage in a non-stick skillet. Cook until all pink color disappears; drain fat. Add wine and cook down until sausage appears glazed. Set aside.

Saute peppers, parsley and garlic in a non-stick skillet sprayed with olive oil until peppers are just tender but still crisp. Add sausage and broth and cook briefly.

Toss pepper and sausage mixture with pasta. Add optional tomatoes. Add salt and pepper to taste, and toss again. Let flavors blend and serve at room temperature.

Serves 6.

Spaghetti, Italian Sausages and Red Peppers in a Sprightly Sauce

*H*ere is a salad to add pep and punch to any menu. It can also stand alone with the help of chewy, crusty bread and a tossed green salad.

16 ounces spaghetti
½ pound sweet Italian sausage, or Italian-seasoned turkey or veal sausage, removed from the casing
2 tablespoons olive oil
3 dried hot chili peppers
1 28-ounce can plum tomatoes, drained and coarsely chopped
3 cloves garlic, minced
2 teaspoons oregano, crushed
Salt and freshly ground pepper (amount will be determined by the seasoning in the sausage)
3 large red peppers, thinly sliced
½ cup chopped parsley
¼ cup coarsely grated Parmesan cheese

Cook pasta until al dente, drain, rinse with cold water and drain again. Transfer to a deep platter or a large shallow bowl.

Heat a non-stick skillet and saute sausage until it loses its pink color. Remove with slotted spoon and discard the fat.

Heat the olive oil, add the chili peppers and saute until they turn black. Discard peppers, save oil. Add the tomatoes, oregano, garlic, salt and pepper to the skillet and simmer 15 minutes. Remove from the heat and stir in the sliced peppers and sauteed sausages.

Add the sauce to the pasta, toss and cool to room temperature. At serving time taste for seasoning and sprinkle with the parsley and Parmesan cheese, toss again and serve.

Serves 6.

Primavera with Italian Sausage

*T*his is not quite an authentic primavera because of the addition of the sausage, but the contrast of the colors makes it an eye- appealing salad.

10 ounces rotelle or other twist pasta
¼ pound sweet Italian sausage
¼ pound hot Italian sausage
½ pound fresh asparagus, cut into 2-inch diagonal pieces
½ pound small mushrooms, left whole or halved
½ box cherry tomatoes, halved if large
½ cup chopped parsley, preferably the flat-leaf variety

Dressing
¼ cup olive or canola oil
¼ cup vegetable broth
3 tablespoons white wine or herb vinegar
2 tablespoons lemon juice
2 cloves garlic, minced
½ teaspoon salt, or more to taste, depending on sausage seasoning
Freshly ground pepper, to taste

Remove sausage from casings and saute until it loses its pink color. Remove with a slotted spoon and set aside to cool.

Cook pasta until al dente, drain and toss with the cooked sausage.

Blanch the asparagus in boiling water for 2 minutes, drain and rinse with cold water. Drain well and pat dry with paper towels.

Add asparagus, mushrooms and tomatoes to the pasta and sausage mixture. Cover and refrigerate until serving time.

In a small bowl, mix the dressing ingredients and set aside. Just before serving, add the parsley and dressing to the salad and toss gently. Adjust seasoning as needed.

Serves 6.

Salad Dressings and Sauces

Salad Dressings and Sauces

*T*hese low-fat and no-fat dressings also are good as toppings on green salads, cold or hot vegetables, or as tasty "skinny" dipping sauces.

Low-Fat Basic Vinaigrette

$\frac{1}{2}$ cup olive or canola oil
1 tablespoon water
$\frac{1}{4}$ cup vinegar
1 teaspoon dry mustard or 2 teaspoons Dijon mustard
$\frac{1}{2}$ teaspoon salt, or to taste
$\frac{1}{2}$ teaspoon freshly ground pepper
Pinch of sugar

Whisk ingredients together in a small bowl.

Yields about $\frac{3}{4}$ cup.

Low-Fat Herbed Vinaigrette

2 tablespoons white wine vinegar
⅓ cup canola oil
1 tablespoon olive oil
1 teaspoon Dijon mustard
1 tablespoon finely chopped parsley
2 teaspoons finely chopped tarragon or 1 teaspoon dried tarragon, crushed
2 teaspoons minced chives
2 teaspoons finely minced basil or 1 teaspoon dried basil, crushed
½ teaspoon salt
Fresh ground pepper to taste, about ¼ teaspoon

In a small bowl whisk the vinegar, mustard, salt and pepper together. Whisk in the oil, then stir in the fresh or dried herbs. Taste for seasoning.

Yields about ½ cup.

Low-Fat Dill Vinaigrette

¼ cup canola oil
¼ cup chicken broth, fat removed, or vegetable broth
3 tablespoons white wine vinegar
1 tablespoon Dijon mustard
½ teaspoon salt
Freshly ground pepper, about ¼ teaspoon
½ teaspoon sugar
3 tablespoons chopped fresh dillweed, or 1 tablespoon dried dillweed

In a small bowl whisk together the vinegar, broth, mustard, salt, pepper and sugar. Add the oil and dill and whisk until well incorporated. Taste for seasoning.

Yields about ¾ cup.

Low-Fat Sesame Seed Vinaigrette

2 cloves garlic, minced
2 teaspoons sesame seeds
¼ cup olive or canola oil
¼ cup chicken broth, fat removed
3 tablespoons wine vinegar
½ teaspoon salt
Freshly ground pepper, about ¼ teaspoon

In a small skillet saute the garlic and sesame seeds in the oil until seeds are lightly browned. Strain the oil into a small bowl and put the garlic and sesame seeds into another small bowl. Add the vinegar, salt and pepper to the garlic and seeds, whisk together. Add the oil and broth and whisk again; taste for seasoning.

Yields about ½ cup.

Low-Fat Tarragon
and Soy Vinaigrette

$\frac{1}{4}$ cup olive or canola oil
3 tablespoons tarragon vinegar
$\frac{1}{4}$ cup chicken broth, fat removed
3 tablespoons soy sauce
1 tablespoon chopped fresh tarragon or 1 teaspoon dried tarragon, crushed
1 teaspoon dry mustard
$\frac{1}{2}$ teaspoon sesame oil (optional)
Freshly ground pepper to taste

Whisk all ingredients together in a small bowl. Taste for seasoning.

Yields about $\frac{3}{4}$ cup.

Fat-Free Mustard Vinaigrette

1 tablespoon Dijon mustard
2 tablespoons apple juice concentrate
2 tablespoons fresh lemon juice
$\frac{1}{2}$ teaspoon basil, crushed
$\frac{1}{4}$ teaspoon oregano, crushed
$\frac{1}{4}$ teaspoon freshly ground pepper
$\frac{1}{8}$ teaspoon salt
$\frac{1}{8}$ teaspoon artificial sweetener

Shake all ingredients together in a covered jar and leave at room temperature at least 2 hours before using.

Yields about $\frac{1}{2}$ cup.

Almost No-Fat
Tomato-Herb Dressing

1 cup tomato juice
¼ cup wine vinegar
1 tablespoon Dijon mustard
½ teaspoon basil, crushed
½ teaspoon oregano, crushed
½ teaspoon ground cumin
½ teaspoon ground coriander
½ teaspoon celery salt
½ teaspoon sugar
2 cloves garlic, minced
2 teaspoons cold water
2 teaspoons cornstarch or arrowroot
1 tablespoon finely minced celery tops
1 tablespoon finely minced green onion tops
1 tablespoon olive or canola oil

In a small saucepan heat all the ingredients except the cold water,
cornstarch, minced celery, onion tops and the oil. Simmer, uncovered,
five minutes. Mix the water and cornstarch together and stir into the
juice mixture; simmer 5 minutes. Set aside to cool. Stir in the minced
celery, onion and oil. Cover tightly and refrigerate. Keeps well.

Yields about 1⅓ cups.

Low-Fat Anchovy Dressing

3 anchovy fillets, drained, chopped
3 tablespoons wine vinegar
1 teaspoon Dijon mustard
$\frac{1}{4}$ teaspoon freshly ground pepper
$\frac{1}{3}$ cup olive or canola oil

Mash the anchovy fillets in the bottom of a small bowl, and whisk in the vinegar, mustard and pepper. Add the oil and mix thoroughly. Taste for seasoning.

Yields about $\frac{1}{2}$ cup.

Low-Fat Sauce Verte

½ cup fat-free yogurt
½ cup low-fat mayonnaise
½ cup chopped parsley
½ cup chopped watercress
1 tablespoon snipped fresh chives, or 1 teaspoon dried chives
2 teaspoons tarragon, crushed
1 tablespoon lemon juice
Salt and freshly ground pepper to taste

Combine all ingredients together in a blender or food processor and blend until smooth. Turn into a small bowl, taste for seasoning, then cover and refrigerate.

Yields about 1¼ cups.

Low-Fat Herb Sauce

1 bunch watercress, coarse stems removed
½ bunch parsley, coarse stems removed
6 green onions, cut into 1-inch pieces
1 tablespoon Dijon mustard
1 teaspoon salt
Freshly ground black pepper to taste
½ cup canola or olive oil
¼ cup chicken broth, fat removed

Wash watercress and parsley and pat dry with paper towels. Add the green onions to the bowl of a food processor and mince. Add the watercress and parsley to the onions and mince. Add the mustard, salt, pepper and with the machine running add the oil in a slow stream. Add the chicken broth and process to blend. The sauce will be thick but if it appears too thick to suit you, add up to 2 more tablespoons chicken broth. Taste for seasoning. Store in a glass or plastic container and cover tightly to prevent discoloration.

The sauce will keep under refrigeration for about 3 weeks and freezes well.

Yields about 1¼ cups.

Low-Fat Creamy Garlic Dressing

½ cup fat-free yogurt
2 tablespoons low-fat mayonnaise
3 tablespoons tarragon or wine vinegar
1 tablespoon olive or canola oil
1 teaspoon salt
¼ teaspoon freshly ground pepper
½ teaspoon sugar
1 teaspoon tarragon, crushed
3 cloves garlic, minced

Add all the ingredients to the bowl of a food processor or blender and blend until creamy.

Yields about 1 cup.

Low-Fat Parsley Pesto

4 cups parsley, coarse stems removed
¼ cup walnut pieces
¼ cup Parmesan cheese
5 cloves garlic, halved
1 teaspoon salt
½ teaspoon freshly ground pepper
½ cup chicken broth, fat removed
¼ cup olive or canola oil

In a food processor or blender process the parsley, nuts, cheese, garlic, salt and pepper. Slowly add the broth and oil and process until well blended. Taste for seasoning.

Yields about 1¼ cups.

Low-Fat Spinach Pesto

1 10-ounce box frozen chopped spinach
⅓ cup chopped parsley
¼ cup grated Parmesan cheese
2 tablespoons pine nuts or walnut pieces
3 cloves garlic, halved
½ teaspoon thyme
½ teaspoon salt
½ teaspoon freshly ground pepper
½ cup vegetable broth
2 tablespoons olive or canola oil

Thaw and squeeze as much water as possible out of spinach. In a food processor or blender mix together the spinach, parsley, Parmesan cheese, nuts, garlic, thyme, salt and pepper. Blend thoroughly until smooth. With the motor running slowly add the broth and oil. Do not continue mixing once the oil has been incorporated. Taste for seasoning.

Sauce will keep about one week, tightly covered and refrigerated, and it can be frozen.

Yields about 1½ cups.

Low-Fat Fresh Spinach and Parsley Pesto

2 cups tightly packed fresh spinach, thoroughly washed and tough stems removed
1 cup parsley, lower stems removed
$\frac{1}{4}$ cup vegetable broth
3 tablespoons olive or canola oil
3 tablespoons freshly grated Parmesan or Romano cheese
3 cloves garlic, halved
1 teaspoon oregano, crushed
1 teaspoon salt
$\frac{1}{2}$ teaspoon freshly ground pepper

Place spinach, parsley, cheese and seasonings in a food processor or blender and process until smooth. With the machine running slowly add the broth and oil. Taste for seasoning.

Before using with pasta or vegetables, add 1 tablespoon of pasta cooking water to amount of pesto being used.

Refrigerate in a tightly closed glass container.

Yields about 1 cup.

Low-Fat Creamy Pesto Sauce

2 cups fresh basil leaves
2 hard-cooked egg whites, quartered
½ cup chicken broth, fat removed, or vegetable broth
2 tablespoons olive or canola oil
3 tablespoon freshly grated Parmesan cheese
2 tablespoons basil or white wine vinegar
3 cloves garlic, halved
1 teaspoon salt
½ teaspoon freshly ground pepper

Place all ingredients except broth and oil in a food processor or blender and process until coarsely chopped. With the machine running slowly add the broth and oil until pureed. Store in a covered glass container in the refrigerator.

Yields about 1¼ cups.

Low-Fat Creamy Dressing

$\frac{1}{2}$ cup fat-free yogurt
$\frac{1}{4}$ cup low-fat mayonnaise
1 tablespoon herb or white wine vinegar
1 tablespoon skim milk
1 teaspoon dry mustard
$\frac{1}{2}$ teaspoon paprika
$\frac{1}{2}$ teaspoon dillweed
$\frac{1}{2}$ teaspoon tarragon, crushed
$\frac{1}{2}$ teaspoon salt
$\frac{1}{4}$ teaspoon freshly ground pepper

Whisk all the ingredients together and refrigerate overnight or a few hours before using. Taste for seasoning.

Yields about $\frac{3}{4}$ cup.

Index

172